The Theatre Student

PRACTICAL STAGE LIGHTING

The Theatre Student

PRACTICAL STAGE LIGHTING

Emmet Bongar

PUBLISHED BY
RICHARDS ROSEN PRESS, INC.
NEW YORK, N.Y. 10010

Standard Book Number: 8239-0224-2
Library of Congress Catalog Card Number: 70-125194
Dewey Decimal Classification: 792

Published in 1971 by Richards Rosen Press, Inc.
29 East 21st Street, New York City, N.Y. 10010

Copyright 1971 by Emmet Bongar

All rights reserved. No part of this book may be reproduced
in any form without written permission from
the publisher, except by a reviewer.

FIRST EDITION

Manufactured in the United States of America

ABOUT THE AUTHOR

EMMET WALD BONGAR is an Assistant Professor of Theatre Arts at Thiel College, Greenville, Pennsylvania, where he directs all campus theatrical activities. He also serves as a technical theatre consultant to educational institutions and community theatres in the design of stages and lighting systems for auditoriums and little theatres.

He holds a B.S. degree in Education, awarded in 1941 by Danbury State College, Danbury, Connecticut, and an M.A., awarded in 1947 by Teachers College, Columbia University, New York City.

Professor Bongar began his theatrical career in 1935 when, as a high-school student, he obtained a job as a part-time stagehand. During his college years he progressed to positions as technician, stage manager, and technical director. Subsequently he served as a student assistant for two semesters in charge of Stagecraft Laboratory at Teachers College, as technical director for the Youngstown Playhouse, Youngstown, Ohio, Kennebunkport Playhouse, Kennebunkport, Maine, and Town and Country Players, Rocky Hill, Connecticut, and as director of the Oak Ridge Playhouse, Oak Ridge, Tennessee, Mt. Lebanon Players, Pittsburgh, Pennsylvania, Manor Players, Howard County, Maryland, and Catonsville Players, Catonsville, Maryland.

In addition, he has acted with the Pittsburgh Playhouse and the Little Lake Theatre, Canonsburg, Pennsylvania, as well as many of the above-mentioned groups.

During World War II Professor Bongar interrupted his career while he served for four years in the U.S. Navy as an Aviation Radioman. Before taking his present position, he worked for fifteen years for Westinghouse Electric Corporation, General Electric Company, Hazeltine Electronic Corporation, and Union Carbide Corporation. Although he has had practical experience in all aspects of theatrical production, his broad background in electricity has served to make him strongest in the area of stage lighting.

In 1949 Professor Bongar married the former Audrey Miller, an accomplished actress and teacher of Speech and Drama. They have two children, Michael and Mary.

PREFACE

Back in the heyday of the "Little Theatre Movement," in the Twenties of our century, England's Norman Marshall made a singular remark about stage lighting that has remained with me all the years of my theatrical experience. As I recall, Marshall said something like this: "It's easy enough to light your stage so that your actors' faces are clearly visible; and it's not so difficult to light a stage to achieve effective stage pictures and what we term 'atmosphere'; but the real test of how good your stage lighting is will be the extent to which it succeeds in combining these two principles."

Forty years later that advice underscores the fundamental approach of Mr. Bongar as he has prepared this book on *Practical Stage Lighting* for amateurs. As an actor and director the author has lived each hectic moment of his sixteen chapters. He writes from the day-by-day adventures that have produced all our theatrical know-how—and he has had the grace and good sense to present his experience in a straightforward and reasonable fashion, which should endear him to what I sincerely anticipate will be a large number of young technicians. Were I once again to find myself in charge of production in a high school or small college, I should hope that not only my technical personnel but all those with any relation to production would read and profit by his words and excellent drawings.

One real value Mr. Bongar's book will have for the amateur is the constant eye he keeps upon the enforced economies of production. All along the way, as he leads his reader casually from one technical complication to another, he not only reminds him of what is merely cheaper to purchase or to build, but he constantly evaluates each item in terms of long-range investment in the securing of an equipment stockpile.

Perhaps the real excitement of this book lies in the quiet way in which Mr. Bongar points the amateur theatre toward experimentation, away from the well-made little comedies in their conventional settings and into the freshness and freedom of arena and thrust staging, the projection of atmospheric scenery, and a legitimate appeal to the eye of properly lighted settings and costumes. At one point he uses his own plans for a successful production of Ibsen's *Peer Gynt* in a way that eradicates fear and distrust of so ambitious a project, persuading his reader that such dramas are well within the reach of the amateur stage.

Above all, Mr. Bongar does not allow his interest in lighting to run away with the show. He believes profoundly in the collaboration between the playwright, designer, director, technical director, and the actors and musicians, as the way to achieve a vital theatrical experience. My hope is that his book will instruct—as it surely must—but also will inspire amateurs to adventure with theatre that appeals to the imaginative experience not by the photographic and the stereotype, that vast kingdom of dullness in all amateur efforts, but through exploration of new forms, new colorings, new textures.

Thiel College

Harry William Pedicord
Chairman, American
   Society for Theatre
   Research

CONTENTS

I.	*Purposes of Stage Lighting*	13
II.	*Applied Electrical Techniques*	17
III.	*Sources of Light*	27
IV.	*Reflectors and Lenses*	31
V.	*Lighting Instruments*	36
VI.	*Care and Maintenance of Lighting Instruments*	53
VII.	*Budget Lighting*	56
VIII.	*Dimmers—Resistance and Auto-Transformers*	63
IX.	*Dimmers—Electronic*	70
X.	*Switchboards and Consoles*	73
XI.	*Budget Controls*	82
XII.	*The Use of Color*	87
XIII.	*Special Effects*	93
XIV.	*Lighting the Proscenium Stage*	97
XV.	*Arena and Thrust Stage Lighting*	101
XVI.	*Lighting Plots and Cue Sheets*	106

Appendices

    A. *The Fundamentals of Electricity*

    B. *Sources of Supply*

Bibliography

ILLUSTRATIONS

Chapter II—*Applied Electrical Techniques*

    Figure 1. Types of screwdriver: (a) stubby (b) jeweler's (c) electrician's (d) standard (e) Phillip's head (Courtesy Garbler-Limber Hardware)   18

    Figure 2. Types of pliers and cutters: (a) gas pliers (b) adjustable pliers (c) long-nose pliers (d) lineman's pliers (e) diagonal cutters (Courtesy Garbler-Limber Hardware)   19

    Figure 3. The adjustable end wrench (Courtesy Garbler-Limber Hardware)   20

    Figure 4. Soldering tools: (top) soldering gun (bottom) soldering iron   21

    Figure 5. Types of connector: (a) parallel blade (b) pin (c) Twist-Lock   23

    Figure 6. Three-wire stranded cable with flexible rubber insulation   24

    Figure 7. Wiring a pin connector   24

    Figure 8. Wiring a Twist-Lock connector   24

    Figure 9. The electrician's knot   25

    Figure 10. Cross section of a wall box showing a stage plug   25

    Figure 11. Wiring a stage plug   25

Chapter III—*Sources of Light*

    Figure 12. The parts of a lamp: (a) bulb (b) filament (c) base   28

    Figure 13. Common filament forms (Courtesy Sylvania Lighting Handbook)   28

    Figure 14. Common bulb shapes (Courtesy Sylvania Lighting Handbook)   29

    Figure 15. Common lamp bases (Courtesy Sylvania Lighting Handbook)   29

Chapter IV—*Reflectors and Lenses*

    Figure 16. Characteristics of a spherical reflector   31

    Figure 17. Characteristics of a parabolic reflector   32

    Figure 18. Characteristics of an ellipsoidal reflector   32

    Figure 19. Refraction of light   33

    Figure 20. Convex lenses: (a) plano-convex (b) double-convex   34

    Figure 21. Cross section of a fresnel lens   35

    Figure 22. Cross section of a step lens   35

Chapter V—*Lighting Instruments*

    Figure 23. Box-type spotlight   37

    Figure 24. Clamps: (a) pipe clamp (b) C-clamp (Courtesy Kliegl Bros.)   37

    Figure 25. 1,000-watt spotlight   38

    Figure 26. Spotlight with cylindrical casing (Courtesy Century-Strand, Inc.)   39

    Figure 27. Fresnel spotlight (Courtesy Century-Strand, Inc.)   40

    Figure 28. Ellipsoidal spotlight (Courtesy Century-Strand, Inc.)   41

    Figure 29. Cross-section view of an ellipsoidal spotlight (Courtesy Century-Strand, Inc.)   42

    Figure 30. Ellipsoidal reflector floodlight or "scoop" (Courtesy Century-Strand, Inc.)   45

    Figure 31. Olivette floodlight   46

    Figure 32. Beam projector (Courtesy Century-Strand, Inc.)   47

    Figure 33. Simple striplight   48

10 / Illustrations

Figure 34.	Modern striplight (Courtesy Kliegl Bros.)	48
Figure 35.	Sciopticon (Courtesy Kliegl Bros.)	49
Figure 36.	Linnebach projector	50
Figure 37.	Cross-section view of a pipe stand	51
Figure 38.	Methods of attaching an instrument to a pipe stand: (a) ½″ pipe screwed directly to yoke (b) ½″ pipe with drilled cap fastened to yoke (c) ½″ pipe with rosette in place of yoke (d) offset ½″ pipe with rosette	51

Chapter VII—*Budget Lighting*

Figure 39.	Plans for a dishpan floodlight: (a) inside of pan—mounting of sockets (b) back of pan—wiring diagram	57
Figure 40.	Plans for a homemade striplight: (a) top view and wiring (b) side view	58
Figure 41.	Plans for a tin can spotlight: (a) side view (b) end view	59
Figure 42.	Pattern for a homemade color frame	60
Figure 43.	Using pipe fittings to mount a spotlight	61

Chapter VIII—*Dimmers—Resistance and Auto-Transformers*

Figure 44.	Diagram of a resistance dimmer	64
Figure 45.	A resistance dimmer without a casing	65
Figure 46.	A bank of resistance dimmers	66
Figure 47.	Principles of the transformer: (a) induction (b) transformer (c) auto-transformer	67
Figure 48.	Auto-transformer dimmers	69

Chapter X—*Switchboards and Controls*

Figure 49.	Types of fuse: (a) plug fuse (b) cartridge fuse (c) circuit breaker	75
Figure 50.	Modern console control board (Courtesy Ward Leonard Electric Co.)	77
Figure 51.	A dimmer unit for a console (Courtesy Kliegl Bros.)	78
Figure 52.	A control unit with a cross-fader (Courtesy Ward Leonard Electric Co.)	79
Figure 53.	The Memo-Q * control unit (Courtesy Century-Strand, Inc.)	80

Chapter XI—*Budget Controls*

Figure 54.	Plans for a salt-water dimmer: (a) tank (b) paddle	84

Chapter XIII—*Special Effects*

Figure 55.	Use of a projected slide for Seal of England effect (*Elizabeth the Queen*, Thiel College)	94

Chapter XIV—*Lighting the Proscenium Stage*

Figure 56.	Acting areas	98
Figure 57.	Method of determining the height of lighting instruments	98
Figure 58.	Method of determining the horizontal position of lighting instruments	98
Figure 59.	Cross-section view of theatre showing location of pipe battens	99
Figure 60.	Top view of characteristic lighting setup	99

Chapter XV—*Arena and Thrust Stage Lighting*

Figure 61.	The "water-tower" approach to thrust and arena lighting	102
Figure 62.	"Clock" approach to thrust and arena stage areas	102
Figure 63.	Typical light plan using "water-tower" lighting	103

* Patent pending.

Figure 64. "Compass-point" approach to thrust and arena stage areas … 103
Figure 65. "Cross-area" lighting for the thrust and arena stages … 104

Chapter XVI—*Lighting Plots and Cue Sheets*

Figure 66. Conventional symbols used in lighting floor plans … 107
Figure 67. Typical lighting floor plan … 108
Figure 68. Typical instrument schedule … 109
Figure 69. Lighting of floor plan for *Peer Gynt* … 110
Figure 70. Instrument schedule for *Peer Gynt* … 113
Figure 71. Typical cue sheet … 114

Appendix A—*The Fundamentals of Electricity*

Figure 72. Diagram of a series circuit … 117
Figure 73. Diagram of a parallel circuit … 118

Chapter I

THE PURPOSE OF STAGE LIGHTING

If someone were to ask you why stage lighting is important to a play, you would undoubtedly reply that without it the audience couldn't see. This spontaneous answer would be the best one. When Edison developed the source for the electric light, no one realized that he had established the groundwork for a future revolution in the art of stagecraft. The earliest records of the theatre show that, since the days of the Greek amphitheatres, darkness and poor visibility had been problems. Many attempts were made to solve those problems, such as using masks and oversized costumes, torches, oil lamps, candles, and gas illumination. It took the electric light, however, to improve upon, or replace, such devices. Throughout the ages the major reason for stage lighting has always been to gain visibility.

The importance of using light for visibility cannot be overstated; but lighting also serves other purposes. The playwright depends upon lighting to help establish the time and place of each scene. The actor knows that good lighting will allow him to use subtle expressions and small, natural gestures and will help him emphasize his important scenes. The modern actor does not use as much exaggeration or other techniques that are considered "hammy," because proper lighting makes such methods unnecessary and obsolete. Designers have found that lighting can make the scenery, properties, and actors look more believable. It also helps the designer set the proper mood and contributes to the overall artistic value of the stage picture. Whether you are called "lighting designer," "technician," "master electrician," or whatever, you are a member of a team that includes the actors, scenery designer, costumer, and sound effects, property, and stage crews. You are just as important to the success of the production as any of the others. Although the full effect of your contribution may not always be apparent to the audience, the other members of your team soon become aware of what the lighting can do for or—in unfortunate cases—to them.

The director, as the leader of your team, is the most concerned about the effectiveness of the lighting, and it is his responsibility to coordinate the lighting with all the other aspects. He makes certain that it does not distract, but contributes to the overall production. The exact organization differs among theatrical groups, but the director is always the leader of the team.

But we have strayed from our discussion of the purposes of lighting. Lighting for visibility is a relative matter. It does not mean flooding the stage with as much brilliant light as can be obtained. It means accenting, or emphasizing, the portions of the stage that are to be used by the actors in displaying the action of the play. This will differ in various theatres, depending upon the distance from the stage to the last row of seats. It also depends upon the viewpoints, or angles, from which the audience can observe the stage. For instance, more powerful lights are required in a large auditorium than would be needed in a small, intimate (200-seat) theatre. A theatre with balconies, or with the audience on more than one side of the stage (see Chapter XV), requires lighting from different angles than would be necessary otherwise. In order to direct and concentrate the light for suitable visibility, the use of spotlights (see Chapter V) is necessary.

Another purpose of stage lighting is to enhance the plausibility of the setting and the actors. Plausibility is determined by whether the lighting is believable to the audience. By using color and special instruments, we can simulate sunlight, moonlight, fireplace glow, candlelight, etc. There are ways, and we will discuss them in later chapters, to show the direction from which the light is supposed to come. For instance, it is possible to give the effect of darkened, or shadowed, sides of actors and objects, yet at the same time light those sides so that the details of form and expression are seen by the audience. Changes in lighting also contribute to plausibility. The switching of a lamp or a wall switch, or the slow change caused by the setting sun can be controlled so as to look believable. Lighting for plausibility makes the viewers more willing to accept what they see on the stage and believe it.

Lighting is also an important means of helping to establish mood on the stage. You can do this by varying the brightness, or intensity, of the lighting and by using colored light. It was known many years before the electric light that brightly lighted scenes instill moods of gaiety and happiness, and dim lighting sets somber, sad, and mysterious moods. Electricity gives us the ability to control with precision the brightness or dimness of the lighting as well as the ability to use and control various colored lights. Color in scenery and costumes had been used for many years to help establish mood, but it could not be used effectively in lighting prior to the use of electric light. Electricity allowed us to use lighting instruments that could safely hold devices to color the light. The ability to use the full spectrum of colored light provides a subtle mood-setting device that may be changed easily and frequently.

Another subtle use of lighting is for the purpose of composition. When we talk about composition, we think of many of the artistic aspects of stagecraft. The chief aspects of composition that lighting affects are called "emphasis" and "picturization." By varying the intensity and the color of the lighting on various parts of the stage, it is possible to point up the most important portions of the stage. This technique causes the audience to pay more attention to those areas. When we use any method to draw the audience's attention to an area or an object, we are using emphasis. The director and the designer are greatly concerned with emphasis. They will indicate where and when to use lights for emphasis. In many cases, however, it will be obvious which is the most important area of the stage.

We use the term "picturization" when we wish to tell a story without depending upon the use of words or sound effects. It is accomplished through the use of scenery, properties, pantomime, and the positions and the intensity of light in certain portions of the movements of the actors, as well as with the lighting. Picturization is achieved by varying stage. A more effective means of picturization through lighting, however, is by the use of color. Most people associate particular colors with specific symbolic meanings. Using light to color the stage, or portions of it, enhances the meaning of the picture. The amount of warmth or coolness of a color also has an effect upon the picturization.

Let us see now what we should remember. First, the purposes of stage lighting are for visibility and artistic considerations. The artistic areas that lighting can best enhance are plausibility, mood, and some aspects of composition. The chief aspects of composition affected by lighting are emphasis and picturization. You may well ask how we can do all that with lights. It is done by the use of certain properties of electric lighting.

Four properties of light and electricity are utilized in stage lighting. They are 1) intensity, 2) color, 3) distribution, and 4) variance (movement). Some of them have been mentioned earlier in our discussion of the purposes of light. Electricity provides the means for controlling those properties. Because we can control them, they can be used to achieve the purposes of stage lighting.

We know that intensity is the brightness of a light. It is measured in units of candlepower and can extend from the extremes of total darkness to blinding brilliance. In order to obtain visibility, a proper amount of intensity is necessary, but too much, and too sudden, intensity must be avoided. Blinding light, obviously, prohibits visibility, whereas sudden changes in intensity require adaptation by the viewer's eyes. You surely have noticed that your eyes take a while to adjust when you go from a lighted room into a darkened area. It is the same principle that makes you squint when you first go out into bright summer sunlight. Thus, intensity changes must allow sufficient time for the audience's eyes to adjust before the play continues. Intensity also has a strong influence upon mood, emphasis, and picturization.

Every color in the spectrum can be produced in the form of a beam of light. Walls, fabrics, and costumes can be made to appear to change color when colored light is reflected from them. It is possible to paint plain surfaces with colored light and have them change colors almost at will before the audience. Colored light may be used to enhance plausibility. It also has an important effect upon mood, emphasis, and picturization.

The term "distribution" covers the direction, size, and shape of the light ray or beam. As in the case of color, control of distribution was virtually impossible before the electric light was invented. It is determined by the type of lighting instrument used and by where that instrument is placed. Most instruments are designed so that the size of the beam may be adjusted, and many have features that allow changes in the shape of the beam as well. Distribution affects all of the purposes of lighting: visibility, plausibility, mood, emphasis, and picturization.

"Variance" is the term used to describe our ability to change intensity, color, and distribution. With the use of electric, and more recently electronic, devices we can quickly change each of the other three properties with precision and selectivity. In most cases, this flexibility is either in the form of movement, or can give the feeling of movement and change. Variance is important to plausibility because it shows the natural, logical development and the constant change in the characteristics of light during the passage of time (for instance, the changing of light from daytime to nighttime). Mood, emphasis, and picturization may be changed quickly or slowly in the view of the audience. In fact, if you wish, you may keep the audience from consciously noticing that a change is being made.

Now that you know the purposes and properties of light, it would be normal for you to shrug it all off as a wondrous subject that only an electrical engineer could understand. Of course, the more you know about the fundamentals of electricity (see Appendix A), the easier it will be for you to understand stage lighting. In order to set and operate a normal stage lighting system, however, all you have to know is how to change a light bulb, turn on a switch, and adjust dials similar to the volume control knob on your television set. On occasion you may need to use a screwdriver or a pair of pliers. The techniques for such tasks are described in the following chapter. No additional skills should be necessary. Your high-school physics course provides more than enough knowledge of electricity, if you wish to understand the theory behind stage lighting.

This introductory chapter has briefly outlined the reasons you should use a proper system to light your stage. You will find that the system and equipment need not be elaborate. Effective and artistic lighting can be obtained with simple, even homemade, equipment. This chapter gives basic lighting design concepts, but is not intended to provide adequate design theory. The remainder of the book provides everything you need to know in order to light the most complicated and most advanced, as well as the simplest, production. It tells you what equipment to use, where to get it, how to use it, and how to make it if you wish to do so. In all cases, do not forget that visibility is the most important purpose of stage lighting. A lighting effect, no matter how dramatic or artistic, is useless if the audience cannot see what is happening onstage.

Chapter II

APPLIED ELECTRICAL TECHNIQUES

Don't let the expression "Applied Electrical Techniques" frighten you. All we will discuss are the simple tools, materials, and devices you will use to make your stage lights operate. We will describe the items and the safe, proper methods of using each one.

As you may know, stage electricians use all sorts of tools such as wire strippers, long-nosed pliers, diagonal cutters, and so forth. For our purpose, however, we can accomplish most of our work with five basic tools. They are 1) a screwdriver, 2) a pair of pliers, 3) an adjustable end wrench, 4) a sharp jackknife, and 5) a soldering tool.

Many types and sizes of screwdrivers are available, but they all consist of three parts—the handle, the shaft, and the head. They can be identified by the type and size of head and by the length of the shaft. The most useful screwdriver for lighting work is usually called an "electrician's screwdriver." It has an insulated handle, as all screwdrivers should. The shaft is 5″ long (an inch longer than the standard screwdriver). The slot-shaped head is ⅜″ wide (the standard is ¼″). Figure 1 gives a comparison of the most common types and sizes of screwdrivers.

In order to work in cramped spaces, you may find it desirable to use a "stubby" screwdriver. It is similar to a standard screwdriver, except that the handle and shaft are shortened, making the overall length 3″. It can be obtained with a head the same width as the electrician's screwdriver.

So many types of pliers exist that it would be confusing to try to discuss them all. Pliers are essentially an electrician's tool, and the more types you have, the easier it will be for you to perform various tasks. For stage work, however, the basic pliers are called "lineman's pliers" or "sidecutters." They are shown in Figure 2. The ends can be used basically for grasping and holding, which are the primary functions of a pair of pliers. The sides can be used to cut wire. Thus, the derivation of the name of sidecutters. If you use pliers without this feature, you will also need a pair of wire cutters. In that case, the most suitable type are called "diagonal cutters." If you have a choice, obtain the 7″ sidecutters and/or the 5″ diagonal cutters. The measurements refer to their overall length.

The adjustable end wrench is more frequently called the "Crescent" wrench because of the trademark given to it by the original manufacturer. It is undoubtedly the most useful tool a stage electrician can have. It is used mostly for adjusting lighting instruments and therefore its use will not be discussed in this chapter. It is, however, an essential tool. Most stage lighting technicians carry one at all times.

An end wrench is a tool that holds and turns nuts and bolt heads. It has, on at least one but usually both ends, an opening of the

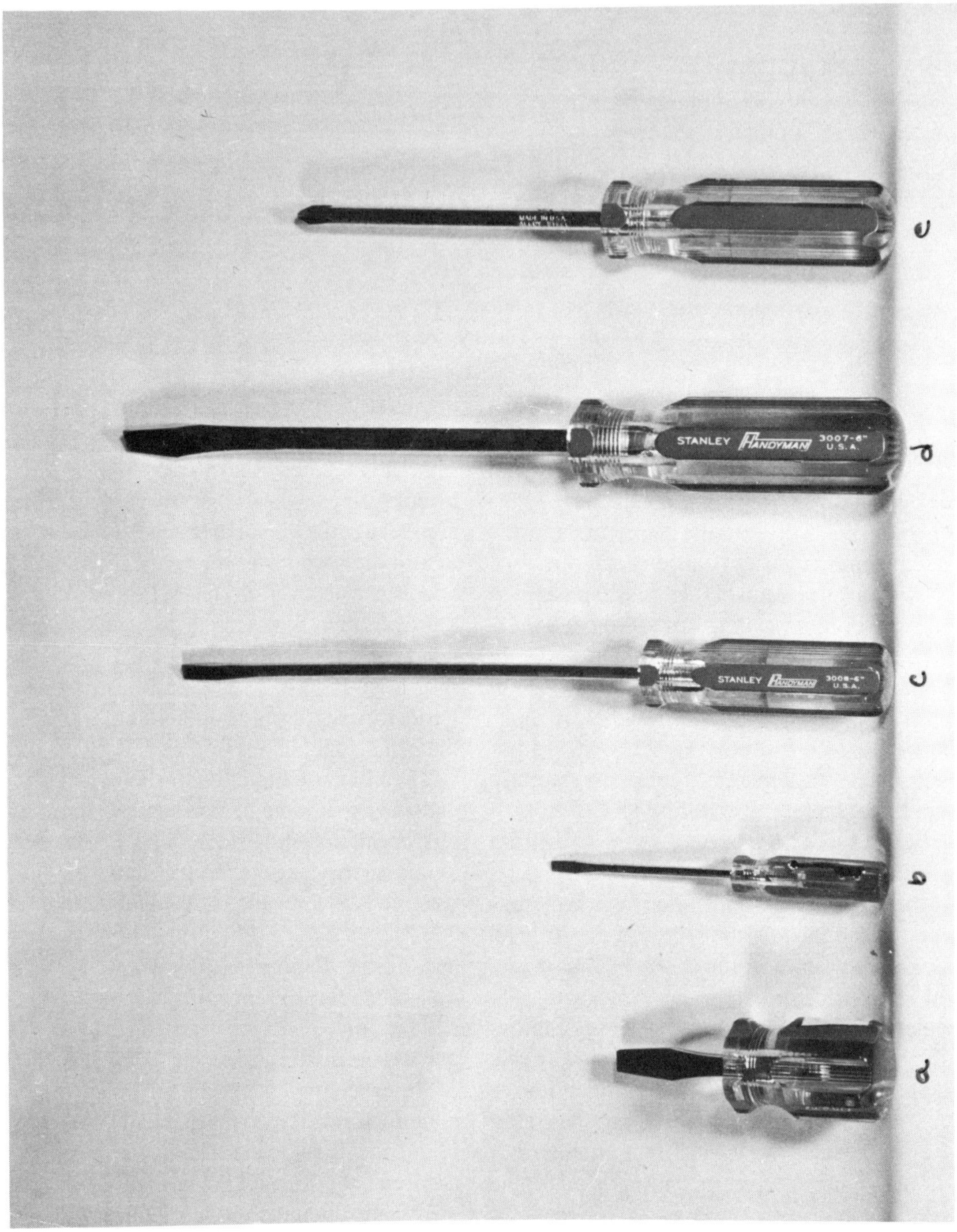

18 / Practical Stage Lighting

Figure 1

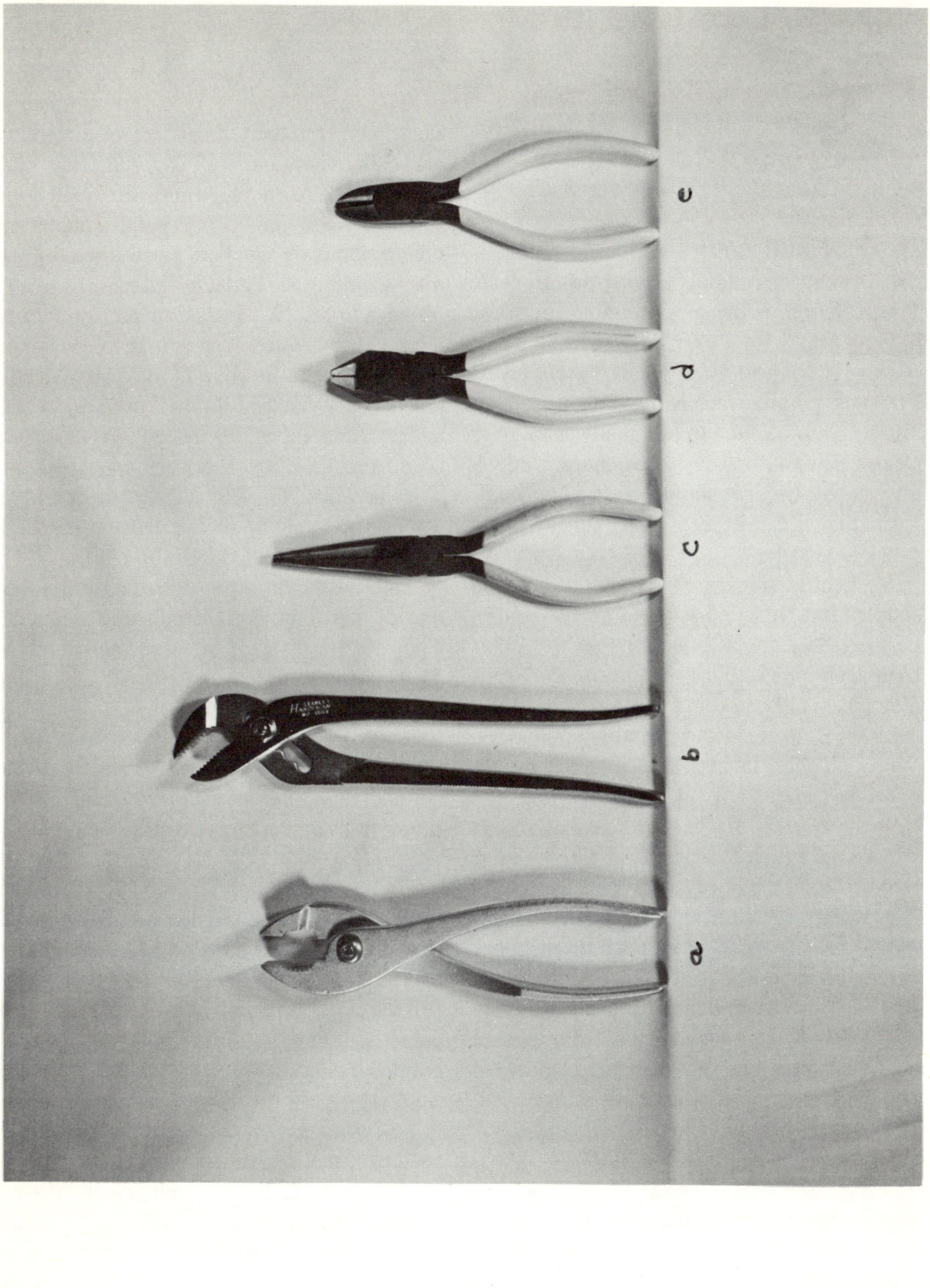

Figure 2

same size and shape of a nut and it comes in sizes to correspond with the various sized nuts and bolts. The adjustable end wrench, as shown in Figure 3, has an opening that

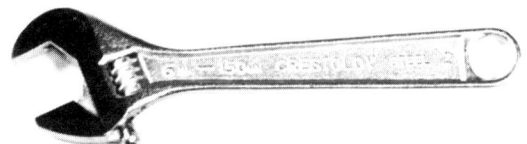

Figure 3

can be adjusted to fit various sized nuts and bolts. It can be obtained in various lengths. The 6″ length is the most suitable for stage lighting use.

Most stage technicians carry jackknives. The most popular type is the four-bladed, or "Boy Scout," knife. It has many uses. For electrical work, however, one sharp blade is all you will need. It should be of good quality so that it can be kept sharp and will not break too easily.

Very little soldering is required for the simple tasks we will discuss. A soldering tool is, therefore, not as necessary as the other tools mentioned above. There are two suitable types: either a soldering gun or a soldering iron. Both are electric heating appliances. When plugged in and turned on, they become hot enough to melt solder. The gun heats up quickly and is more easily handled when you are doing precision work. Since you will have no occasion to perform precision work, the iron is quite satisfactory. It can be held in a vise or propped on the work bench, giving you a free hand at times when you will need all the hands you can get. Figure 4 shows examples of the two types of soldering tool. The 200-watt heavy-duty, or commercial, type of either tool is more suitable for the simple soldering work we will discuss later in this chapter.

Tools should be of good quality. Look for trade names such as Stanley, Craftsman, Fall River, and Crescent. An unknown brand may not be the bargain it appears to be if it breaks easily, becomes dull, or is inaccurate. Secondly, tools must be properly cared for.

Choose high and dry storage space and keep them there when not in use. Keep them clean and dry. Rust on tools can be cleaned with machine oil.

Every material you can think of, whether solid, liquid, or gaseous, can be classified based upon its ability to carry or to resist electricity. The better carriers of electricity are called conductors. The materials that successfully resist electricity are called insulators. Most metals are good conductors. Glass, porcelain, rubber, plastics, cloth, and air are among the better insulators.

Stage lights, like any electrical appliances, must be connected to a source of power in order to work. In your home you plug the toaster or TV set into a wall plug or "receptacle." Sometimes you need an extension cord to make it reach. Since our stage lights must be portable, you will find it necessary to have a supply of such extension cords on hand. They are called lighting cables.

Lighting cables are usually larger than extension cords in both length and diameter. They are made of copper wire to conduct the electricity and are insulated with cloth and rubber. All conductors must be insulated to protect those who may come in contact with them and to keep them from contacting other conducting material (shorting out), which blows fuses and creates extreme heat and fire hazard.

Do not use household extension cords for stage lights. They are not large enough to carry the required current and are liable to overheat, creating a fire hazard. Number 14, two-wire (or three-wire) stranded electrical cable with flexible rubber insulation is preferable. You can use Number 16 (one size smaller) safely for a 500-watt light or less.

Solder is a conducting material that is used to fasten or "solder" two other conductors together. You can melt it with the extreme heat created by a soldering tool. Any such connection must be physically strong before applying the solder. Make sure you use resin core, not acid core, solder for electrical use.

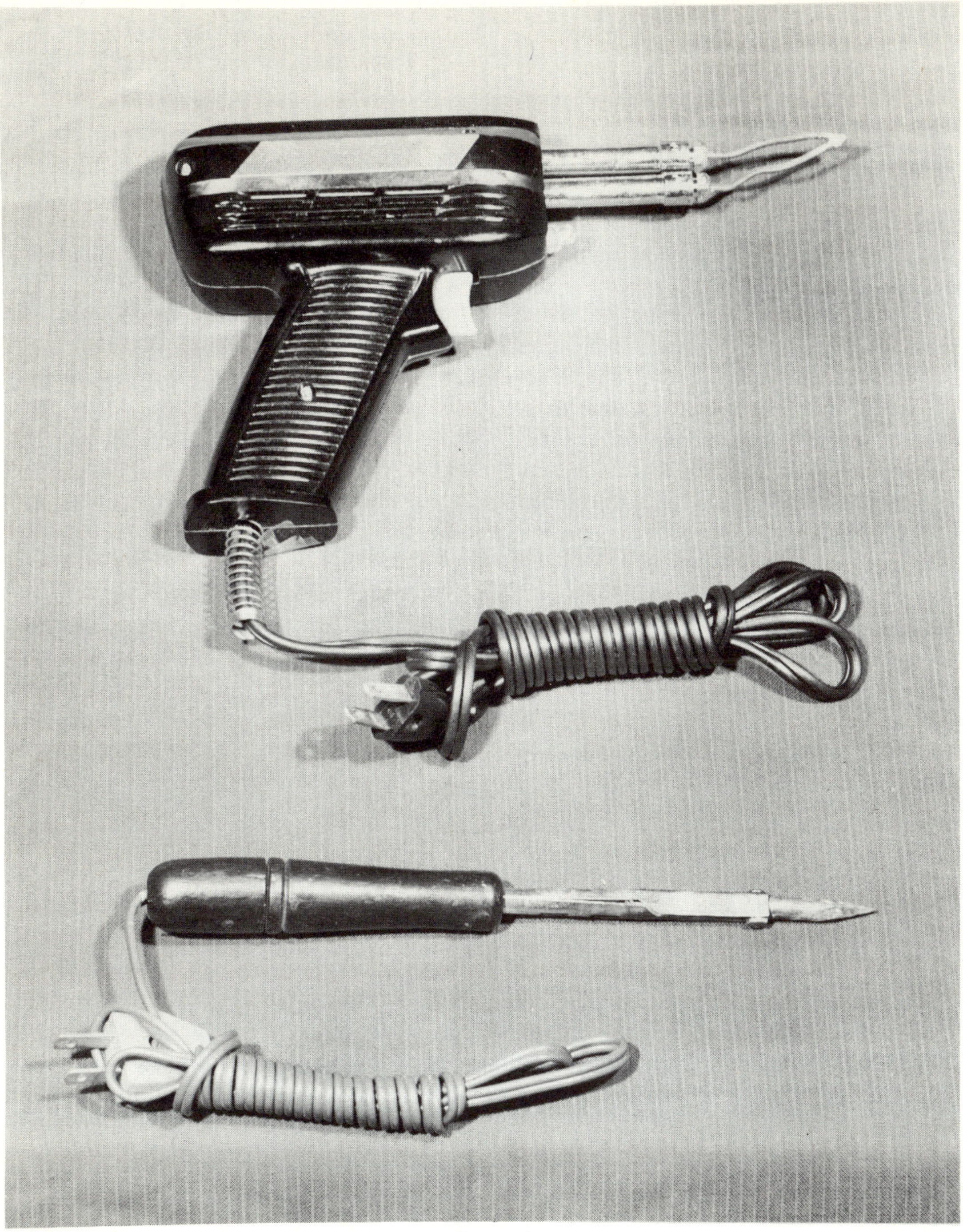

Applied Electrical Techniques / 21

Figure 4

Resin paste is a greasy substance sometimes referred to as "flux." It will help you to melt the solder faster and more evenly. You can also use it to clean the soldering tool.

Tape is used to insulate any exposed section of conductor. The three common types are: rubber tape, friction tape, and plastic tape. Rubber tape adheres only to itself. It is very flexible and pliable, but not very durable. It is a very good insulator and is wrapped around the exposed wire. Friction tape sticks to all types of insulators, rubber, cloth, and itself. It is tough and durable. It is wrapped around the rubber tape to protect it and hold it in place. Friction tape has insulating capability, but it is not a good enough insulator to be used by itself. Plastic tape has the qualities of both rubber and friction tapes. You will probably prefer it because it eliminates the need for two separate rolls of tape. Always wrap your tape as tightly and neatly as possible.

Do not use substitutes or improper materials. You will find it more costly in time and dollars in the long run.

In our discussion of electrical devices, we will not include those devices that are parts or components of lighting instruments and controls. We will discuss such parts or components when we talk about the major instrument itself. The devices we will discuss in this chapter are connectors and plugs.

Lighting instruments, like other appliances, must be easily relocated. Our lighting cables must have devices on each end that will allow us to make quick, secure connections. We call these devices "connectors." The three common types of connectors are as follows: 1) parallel blade, or Edison, connector, 2) pin connector, and 3) Twist-Lock connector.

You are undoubtedly familiar with the Edison connector. This is the common household type, and almost every electric appliance uses this type of connector. They are not suitable for stage use because they become disconnected too easily, they break easily, and they have limited capacity.

Pin connectors (see Figure 5), have had wide theatrical use for many years. They usually fit so loosely that they fall apart, or so tightly that it is necessary to pry them apart with a tool. When they are loose, they do not make good electrical contact. They can be adjusted (as we shall explain later) to compensate for looseness, but the adjustment tends to increase their resistance to the electrical current.

The Twist-Lock connector (see Figure 5) is a patented device manufactured by Harvey Hubbell, Inc. It has been copied by other manufacturers with varying degrees of success. This connector has inverted L-shaped curved blades that are locked into place by twisting the connector after insertion. This, in my opinion, is the most suitable connector for stage use. Although it is more expensive than the unsuitable Edison connector, its price is comparable to the more commonly used pin connector.

All connectors come in pairs, male and female. The opposite ends of each cable must carry mating connectors. You will probably use the two-blade connector. Each type, however, also comes in the three-blade style in the event that you have a three-wire, rather than a two-wire, system. In such a case, make sure that all of your cables are three-wire, not two-wire.

Now that we have described the tools, materials, and devices, let us consider how we are going to use them. The first thing to learn is how to pare the end of a cable. If you have wire strippers, there is nothing to discuss. Just insert the end of the cable in the proper size hole in the strippers, then squeeze the tool, twist the wire, and pull. You have pared, or cleaned, the insulation off the end of the cable.

If, like most of us, you do not have strippers, you will use your knife. The first step, before cutting anything, is to make certain that you know where both ends of the cable are. That way you can make sure that the other end is not connected to a power source and you will not have a shocking experience. Next, about 1″ from the end, start cutting the outermost rubber shield. Cut around the complete diameter first. When you have done that, you will be able to pull the shield off the end of the cable like a small tube or sleeve. This sleeve will be made of rubber unless the cable is attached to a lighting instrument. In that case the outermost insulation will be a woven asbestos material for protection against the heat of the instrument. The asbestos sleeve is removed in the same way.

After you have removed the outer insula-

Applied Electrical Techniques / 23

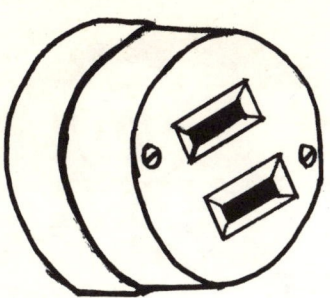 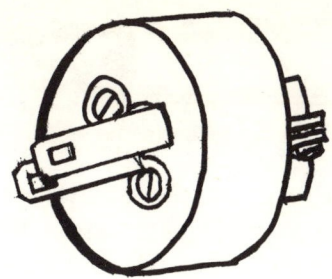

a.

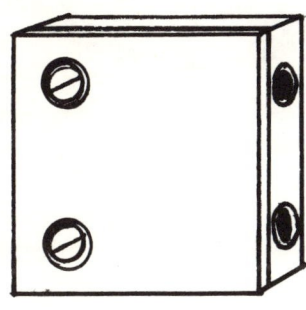 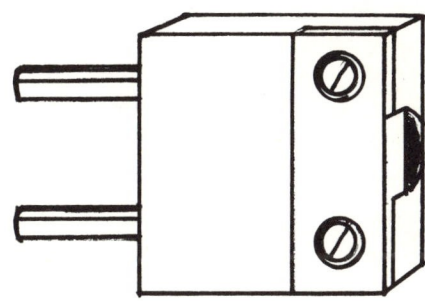

b.

 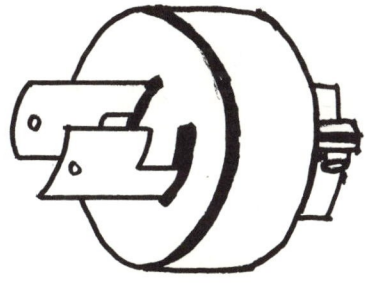

c.

Figure 5

tion, you will see two insulated wires and two pieces of twine or hemp (see Figure 6). The twine is there to help keep the circular shape of the cable, and you may cut it off immediately at the same point where you have pared the outer shield. The two wires are usually colored white and black (or red) for easy identification. If it is a three-wire system, the third is frequently green, although some cable manufacturers make them white, black, and red. Using the same cutting method as before, the colored insulation is removed from each of the wires approximately ¼" from their ends. Take special care not to cut the stranded wire conductor that you will expose as you cut.

24 / Practical Stage Lighting

Figure 6

You may find that the exposed wire conductor is discolored from contact with the rubber insulation. If so, use your knife blade to gently scrape away the discoloration until the wire gleams like new. Before attaching the connector, it is advisable to "tin" the ends of the wire. "Tinning" is the process of coating the stranded ends of the wire with a thin layer of solder to keep them from parting or fraying when bent.

Before tinning you should twist the stranded wire tightly. Do this in a clockwise rotation as you face the cut end. After twisting, cover the wire with resin flux and heat it by applying it directly to the heating element of your soldering tool. Use your pliers to hold the wire firmly. Make sure that the tool has reached its maximum heat level and allow the wire to remain in contact until you feel that the heat has radiated through its diameter. The resin flux will appear to have boiled away. Next, apply the solder to the wire (not to the tool), allowing a small portion of the solder to melt on the wire. Turn the cable while doing this and allow the molten solder to flow between all of the strands. Remove it from the hot tool and gently shake away any excess solder into a metal or asbes-

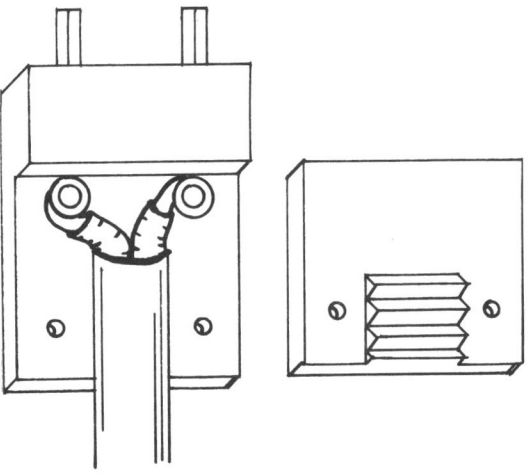

Figure 7

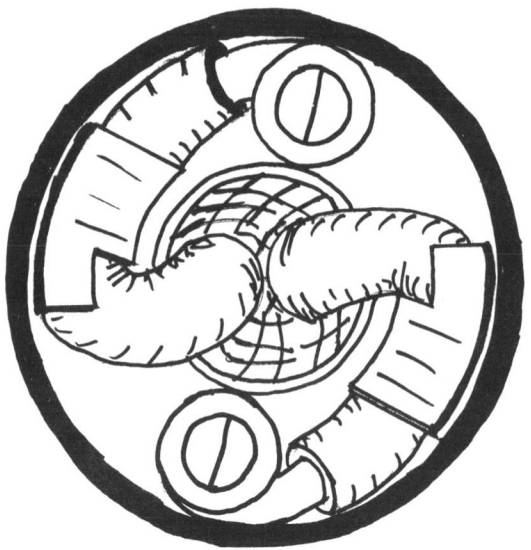

Figure 8

tos tray. When it cools, you should have a thin plating on the surface of the wire and all of the strands. This will hold the strands to one another and make the exposed wire stiff. It is now ready to be attached to the connector.

In view of the rough usage to which lighting cables are subjected, connectors must be firmly attached. Obviously, they must also be well connected electrically to assure continuous flow of current whenever you need it.

Pin connectors and Twist-Lock connectors have features that cause all physical stress and strain to be taken by the outer insulation of the cable if properly attached. Figure 7 shows the proper attachment to a pin connector. Notice the teeth on the inside of the cover, which are intended to bite into and hold the outer insulation. When you pare the end of the cable, measure your cut so that the outer insulation will remain under those teeth. It is a good practice to wrap four or five layers of friction tape tightly around the outer insulation where the teeth will come in contact with it. This will increase the bite and strengthen the connection. If you use the thinner plastic tape, eight or nine layers may be necessary.

In connecting the conductor, you will make what is known as a pressure connection. Each conductor has two screws as shown in Figure 7. The screws have broad, flat heads to press against the wire. Wind the tinned wire around the screw and, using your screwdriver, tighten the head down on the wire. Always wind the wire clockwise so that when you tighten the screw it will tend to tighten, not loosen, the wire. If the wire is not tinned, you will have to take special care to ascertain that all strands are captured underneath the screwhead.

The same principles apply when attaching a Twist-Lock connector. In addition, make sure that you turn each of the two insulated wires around the base of the prongs (or plates) as shown in Figure 8 before making the pressure connection. The Twist-Lock connector has a clamping device on the rear that tightens over the outer insulation for a strong physical connection. Again, in this case, make sure you have cut the end of the cable so that the outer insulation remains under the clamp. As in the case of the pin connector, tape the clamped area of the cable to strengthen the connection.

Since pin connectors sometimes become loose and fall apart, technicians always use an "electrician's knot" when they connect two cables, as shown in Figure 9. Although the same problem does not exist when using Twist-Lock connectors, the electrician's knot should still be used if possible. Note in Figure 7 that the pins on the male pin connector are split. When the connector fits too loosely, it can be tightened by prying the halves of each pin apart with a knife blade or screwdriver. Be careful not to scratch the surface of the pins. The pins should be kept

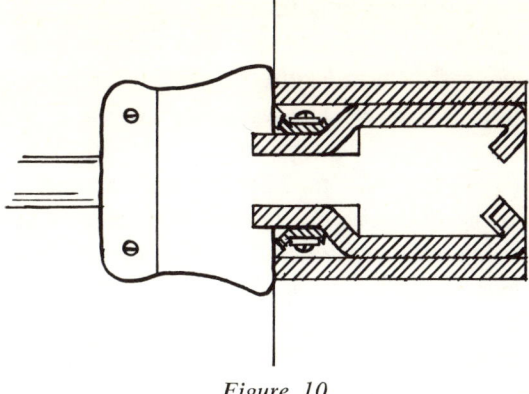

Figure 10

clean. Do not use any cleansing substance or oil. Emery cloth or fine garnet paper are usually satisfactory to clean the surface of the pins.

Mention should be made of another device called the stage plug. Although still in use, it is gradually becoming obsolete. Many stages, however, still have floor boxes and wall boxes. These are receptacles in the floor or wall that form a rectangular opening when their lids are raised. The two opposite sides of each of these openings are connected to an electrical circuit so that when a stage plug is inserted (see Figure 10) the current will be carried through the cable attached to the stage plug. The cable is connected to the stage plug in the same way that you would

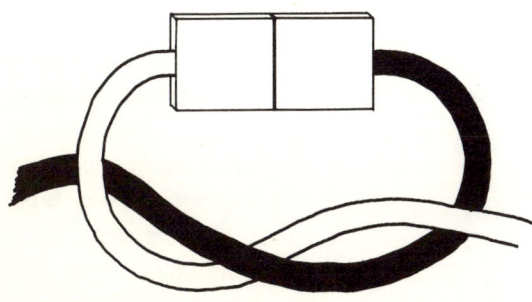

Figure 9

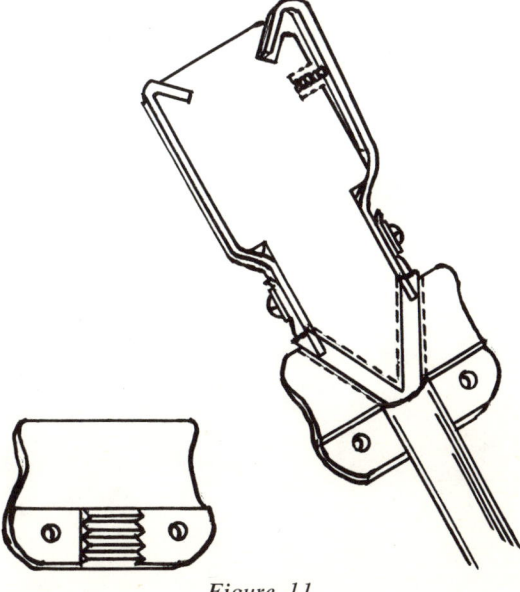

Figure 11

attach it to a pin connector, except that the pressure connections are exposed on each side as shown in Figure 11, instead of being under the cover. The foregoing are the most common electrical practices that you will need to set your stage lights. Other practices will be discussed in the chapters pertaining to lighting instruments and controls. We have hardly scratched the surface of the list of electrical practices that an electrician must know. We have, however, covered the most frequently encountered practices for the stage. If you have any problems or work beyond their scope, you should call in a qualified stage electrician.

Our discussion of electrical practices would not be complete without mentioning the *National Electrical Code* and safety. The "Code" is published by the National Fire Protection Association, a nongovernment group. It is revised every three years. It is a lengthy legal document containing a section on theatrical wiring practices and equipment. It is not national law, although most state or local governments have given it legal status in their building codes and regulations. Copies are usually available in the local library or may be purchased by writing to the National Fire Protection Association, 60 Batterymarch Street, Boston, Massachusetts 02110.

An organization connected with the National Fire Protection Association is the Underwriters' Laboratories, Incorporated. The latter organization tests electrical equipment and material for safety. They allow the manufacturer to use their "UL" label on equipment and material that meets their minimum requirements. Do not use or buy any equipment, material, or device unless it carries the "UL" label.

We cannot say enough concerning safety when using electricity. Electricity can produce enough heat to destroy material, equipment, and buildings. It can cause shocks that can kill and maim. It can set off major explosions. Even the common household variety of electricity can do all of that. On the stage many precautions are necessary. The following are basic:

1. Make sure both sides of a circuit are disconnected before you work on it.
2. Insulate all exposed conductors and connections.
3. Tighten all connections and keep them tight.
4. Look for the "UL" label. No bargain is worth sacrificing this requirement.
5. Do not overload a circuit (this will be explained in Chapter X, "Switchboards and Controls").
6. Keep all material and equipment dry and away from water.
7. When in doubt, call a qualified electrician.

Chapter III

SOURCES OF LIGHT

What do you think of when you hear the word "light"? The sun? A fire? A light bulb? A candle? All are sources of light. Without a source there can be no light. The source is the most important part of a lighting instrument. The source alone can emanate light, but without the source the instrument remains dark.

The source of light in a lighting instrument is what most people, incorrectly, call a "light bulb." Electricians call it a "lamp." A lamp has three major parts: the filament, the bulb, and the base (see Figure 12).

Do you remember what we said about materials and their varying degrees of ability to conduct electricity? Some are good conductors, some are poor, and some are in between. We said that most metals are good conductors. Gold is one of the best, but it is too expensive. That is why we usually use copper. Some of the other metals, though they conduct electricity, do not do so as readily as others. We say that they offer more resistance to the electrical current. The resistance causes friction, which, in turn, creates heat. It is the same principle as a short circuit or poor connection, which you know also offers resistance to electricity, causing heat and producing friction. When we cause electricity to flow through certain metals, it causes so much heat that the metal glows or burns. As you know, many metals can withstand great heat and can burn or glow a long time before they will melt or break. Our friend Thomas Edison found that one of the best of them is tungsten.

Another factor that you should know is that the smaller the diameter of the wire, the more resistance it will offer to an electrical current. If we, therefore, take a piece of very thin tungsten wire and attach it to an electrical circuit, it will glow brilliantly and become a source of light. In order to obtain a maximum amount of light, we coil the wire or bend it into certain shapes as shown in Figure 13.

We call these configurations of wire "filaments." Some of these shapes cast light efficiently in almost all directions. Other shaped filaments can concentrate the light more efficiently in one or two specific directions. By referring to Figure 13, you can probably figure out for yourself why filaments C-7A and C-5 are better for throwing general light in many directions, whereas filaments C-13 and C-13D are more efficient in one or two specific directions.

You may wonder why we don't just use a filament without any glass around it. Here, two factors are involved: insulation and durability. You must remember that there is an electric current flowing through the filament. We must insulate it and yet we must not block the light or create a fire hazard. It is really a relatively easy problem if you remember that glass is one of the good insulators. It has sufficient heat resistance, and we can all see that glass is translu-

28 / **Practical Stage Lighting**

Figure 12

cent. Therefore, we wrap the filament in glass and we have solved the problem of insulation.

Durability, however, is not quite that easy. Although tungsten is one of the most durable metals that can be used as a filament, it still breaks in a relatively short time when subjected to the extreme heat that is generated. The life span of the filament, however, can be greatly extended if it is contained in a vacuum or in certain gaseous environments. The glass insulator, therefore, is shaped into a "bulb" that contains the vacuum, or gas, environment. Just as we have variously shaped filaments, we also have variously shaped bulbs to suit varying purposes. These are shown in Figure 14.

The bulbs you will use most frequently for stage lighting are identified in Figure 14 as "PS," "A," "T," "G," and "PAR." The PS bulbs are pear-shaped and we use them in some floodlights. We use A bulbs mostly in striplights. The T bulbs are tubular and are used in spotlights and projection instruments. We also use the globular G bulbs in spotlights, but they are more commonly found in floodlights. Lamps with PAR bulbs could be called lighting instruments in themselves and we will discuss them and their parabolic shape in Chapter V when we discuss the other types of lighting instruments mentioned above.

The third remaining part of a lamp is the base. The base does more than just hold the filament inside the bulb. It becomes the part of the electrical circuit that connects the filament with the conductor that carries the current to the lighting instrument. In an ordinary household lamp, the base is the portion of the lamp that screws into the light socket. Figure 15 shows styles and sizes (not to scale) of lamp bases. Many of them probably look familiar to you. You should recognize the "candelabra" as being used on Christmas tree lights and the "single contact bayonet candelabra" as the type used in some flashlights. Perhaps you can identify some of the others.

The types we use in stage lighting lamps are: medium screw base, medium prefocus, mogul screw base, mogul prefocus, medium bipost, mogul bipost, and screw terminal.

You can probably figure out for yourself that the terms "medium" and "mogul" refer to size. The remainder of the titles describe the shape or style of base. The sizes range as follows from small to large: miniature, candelabra, medium, and mogul. The term "profocus" is used for the "bayonet" type of base. Technically speaking, the "bipost" base is also for a prefocus type of lamp.

You are undoubtedly most familiar with the medium screw base that is used on the ordinary household lamp. The button on the bottom connects one end of the filament to the circuit; the outer metal casing that is

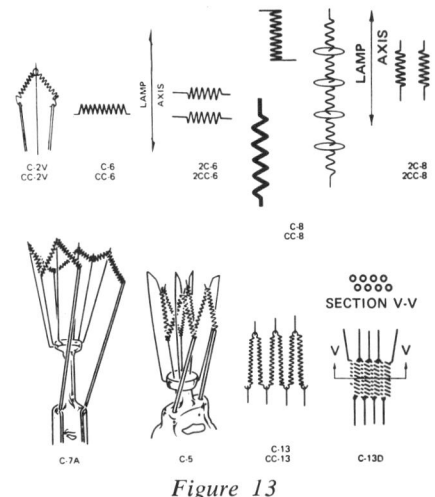

Figure 13

Sources of Light / 29

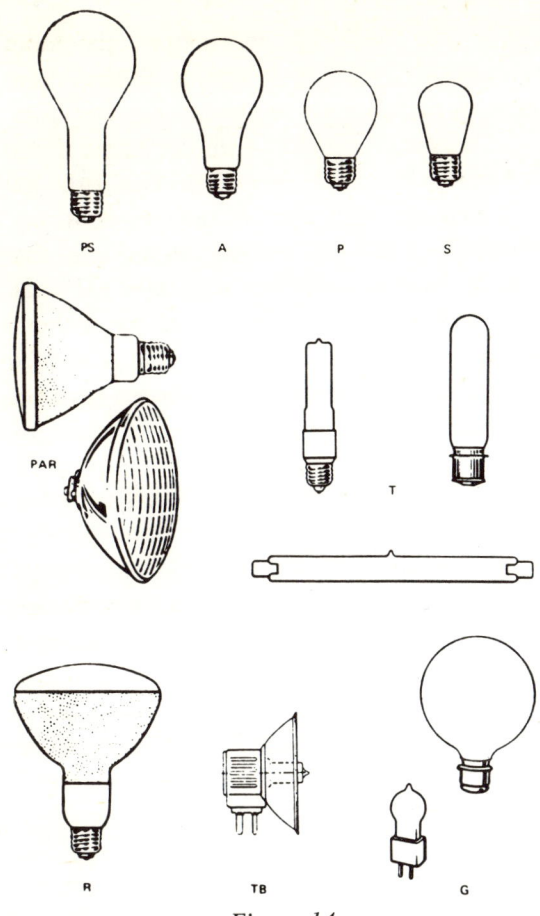

Figure 14

socket. We use this base most frequently in spotlights and projection equipment of 750 watts or less.

The size of the base is increased from medium to mogul if the wattage exceeds 750 watts. You will occasionally find 500-watt and 750-watt lamps that have mogul bases, and some 1,000-watt globular lamps have medium bases.

The medium and mogul bipost bases operate on the same principle as the pin connectors. Although these lamps are usually clamped, or screwed, in place, the posts, or pins, do not wear loose as is the case with pin connectors. The reason is that, once a lamp is placed in its socket, it remains there and is not subjected to the wear that a pin connector encounters. Some bipost bases have one post slighty thinner than the other, when the filament is shaped to direct light in one direction only. Thus it is impossible to insert the lamp backwards. We use the bipost base mostly in ellipsoidal spotlights, which will be described in Chapter V.

The screw terminal, which is found most frequently on automobile headlights, is the least common type of base of those used for

screw-shaped to fasten the lamp in its socket also serves to connect the other end of the filament to the circuit. The material separating the two pieces of metal is a porcelain and/or glass insulator. On the stage you will find the medium screw base in striplights, most floodlights, and some spotlights. It is not frequently used for wattages over 750.

The medium prefocus, or bayonet, base differs from the medium screw base in that the outer metal casing is smooth rather than screw-shaped and it has one, or two, pins extending from it at a right angle. The pin, or pins, fit into L-shaped slots in the socket and when fully inserted and twisted, they lock the lamp in place. It is the same principle as the Twist-Lock connector. The portion of the socket that presses against the button on the bottom of the base has a tension spring behind it in order to maintain pressure to hold the lamp securely in the

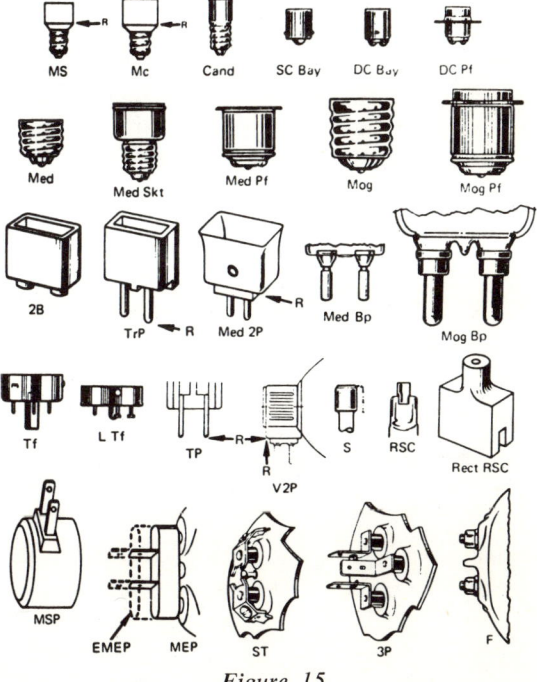

Figure 15

stage lighting. You will find that it is bothersome to try to change this type of lamp quickly since you must use a screwdriver to connect and disconnect each of the terminals separately. All of the other bases described above can be screwed or plugged in and out with relative ease. At least one lighting manufacturer, however, has produced a floodlight that requires a PAR-type lamp with a screw terminal base. Needless to say, that particular lighting instrument offers disadvantages.

We have mentioned the fact that certain filaments are shaped to operate more efficiently in specific directions. We use those filaments in conjunction with prefocus, bayonet, or bipost bases. We do so because those bases automatically position the filament in the lighting instrument so that the strongest light is beamed in the correct direction inside the instrument. The positions of the slots for the pins in the bayonet sockets and the positions of the post holes in the bipost sockets are the key factors in controlling the position of the filament.

Another factor that you should know is that some filaments will burn properly in one position only. Because of this, they are designed to burn in either an upright position or an upside-down position. Lamp manufacturers designate which lamps are to "burn base down" and which are to "burn base up." Failure to "burn" a lamp in the correct position results in a greatly reduced life span. When you order lamps, make sure that you check the location of the lamp socket in your lighting instrument and specify which type you want.

The latest development in lamps is the quartz lamp. Its proper names are the "Quartz-Halogen" or "Tungsten-Halogen" lamp. Its principle, without getting too technical, is based upon the use of a small amount of iodine enclosed in a small transparent quartz container. The heat generated vaporizes the iodine. The vapor increases the efficiency of the lamp and extends the life span of the filament. They burn equally well whether the filament is upright or upside down. We have also found that the quartz lamp produces more efficient colored light in the cooler, or blue, end of the color spectrum.

Originally, quartz lamps required special sockets, and it was necessary to buy expensive adapters or conversion kits in order to use them in our standard lighting equipment. New lighting equipment is now available containing quartz lamp sockets. At least one theatrical lighting manufacturer, Century-Strand, Inc., also produces quartz lamps installed inside of regular bipost and bayonet base lamps, thereby avoiding the need for adapters.

Although quartz lamps cost approximately twice as much as the older type, they last more than four times as long. By using them you can reduce your overall lamps costs and have more efficient light sources.

Chapter IV

REFLECTORS AND LENSES

Let us take a look at what we have covered thus far. We have discussed, among other things, the two basic ingredients necessary in order to create light. Those ingredients are 1) the ability to conduct an electric current properly to the place in which it is to be used, and 2) the ability to convert the electric current into an efficient source of light. We can now proceed to the devices that can be used to direct, control, intensify, and dramatize the light.

In the preceding chapter you read that the shape of the filament can affect the direction of the light. Although this is true, you will find that some light beams will emanate in all directions from a filament regardless of its shape. Since we wish to make use of the light that shines in the wrong direction, we use a reflector.

A reflector is a piece of metal installed behind, or around, a lamp in order to recast, or reflect, the light rays in the desired direction. The surface of the reflector that faces the lamp is usually polished to a mirrorlike sheen in order to intensify and magnify the reflected light to the greatest extent possible. Although reflectors are of most importance in spotlights, they are also used in floodlights and striplights.

The use of reflectors is important to you as a lighting technician because we have discovered that variously shaped reflectors can throw beams of light with special characteristics. If we use a spherical-shaped reflector, the position of the light source in relation to the center of the sphere becomes an important factor, as shown in Figure 16. If the source is situated at the center, all reflected light returns through the source and results in light that is evenly scattered in all reflected directions.

If the source is situated between the reflector and the center, the reflected light beams are concentrated in a center beam

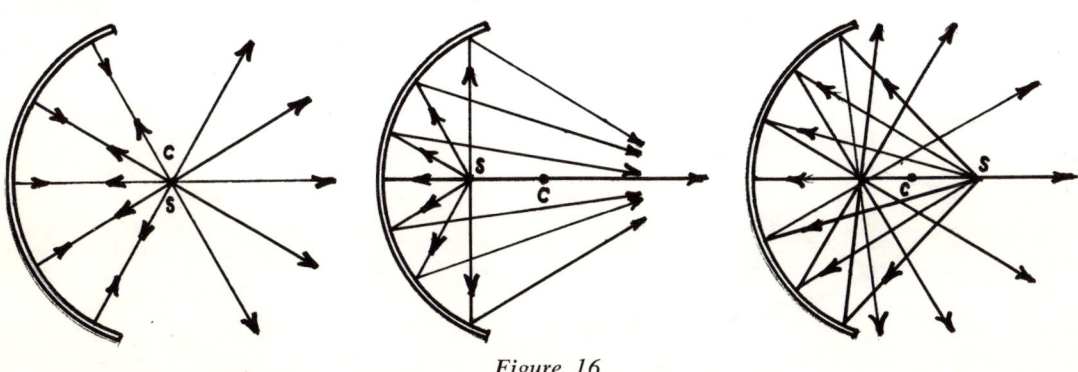

Figure 16

32 / **Practical Stage Lighting**

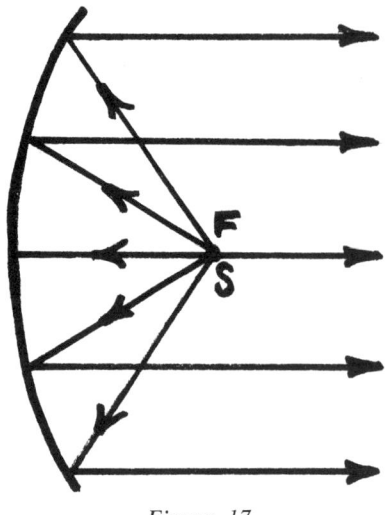

Figure 17

verge. When using a spherical reflector, the focal point is at the center of the sphere, but the light will not be reflected through the focal point unless the source is placed at the sphere's center. If you examine Figure 16, you will see how the reflected rays behave to cause this condition.

We also use reflectors that are parabolic in shape. Figure 17 shows how the parabolic reflector reflects light rays that are parallel to one another when the light source is at the reflector's focal point. You may already know that the ellipsoidal-shaped reflector is used frequently in spotlights. When the source of light is situated at the focal point of the ellipsoidal reflector, as shown in Figure 18, all reflected rays are diverted through a second focal point in front of the source of light. This characteristic has advantages for spotlights that we will discuss in Chapter V.

Thus far, by using a source of light and a reflector, we can direct light in the general area, or direction, that we intend to illuminate. The most complicated household lighting fixtures seldom consist of more than a lamp and a reflector. Some modern fixtures have parabolic or ellipsoidal reflectors, but they are generally chosen for their appear-

that will be brighter than the outer ring of light, which comes only from the unreflected rays that shine directly from the source of light. On the other hand, if the center of the sphere is between the source and the reflector, you get the opposite effect. The reflected light is concentrated around the outer rim of the light beam, and the outer ring of light will be brighter than the center of the beam.

You will find that reflected rays of light may have a focal point. A focal point is a spot where the rays of light all meet, or con-

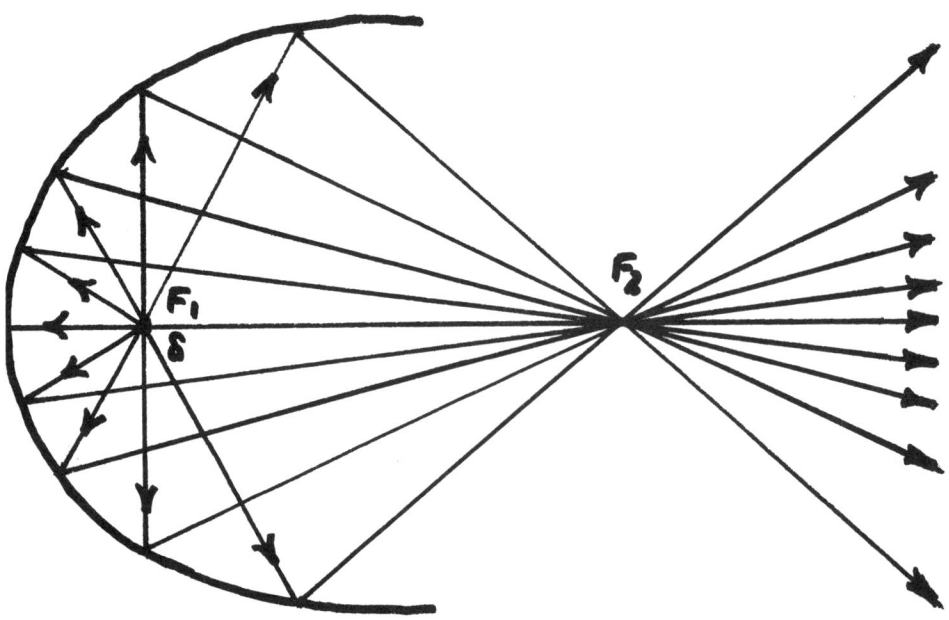

Figure 18

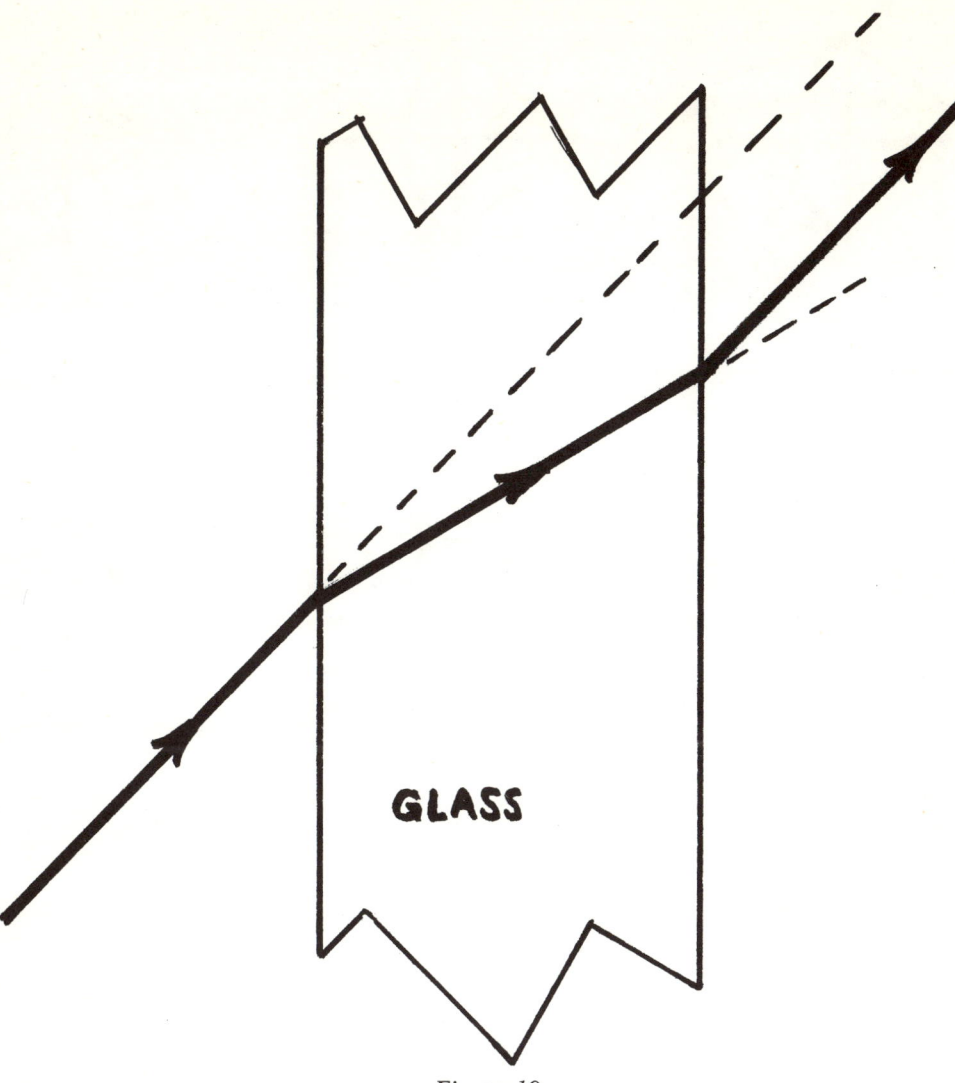

Figure 19

ance rather than their reflective characteristics. On the stage, however, you will want to concentrate, intensify, and even magnify the light beams to a greater degree than is possible by merely using a reflector. To accomplish this we use lenses.

A lens is a glass disc that is shaped so that it will bend, or refract, the rays of light that pass through it. You must have noticed, at some time or other, that if you place a straight stick in water, the stick appears to be bent where it meets the surface of the water. We know that the stick is not actually bent, but the appearance is caused by the fact that the light rays between our eyes and the immersed portion of the stick bend when they go through the water. We call this phenomenon "refraction." It works with glass as it does with water. The direction and degree to which the light rays are bent will depend upon the shape of the glass.

In Figure 19 you can see how a ray of light is bent upon entering a piece of glass and then bent again as it passes through the back surface of the glass. Also note that the ray leaving the glass is parallel to the ray entering the glass. You will find that to be true if the front surface of the glass is parallel to the back surface. Other conditions may be created in which the two surfaces are not parallel. The lenses we use in stage lights have surfaces that are not parallel.

34 / **Practical Stage Lighting**

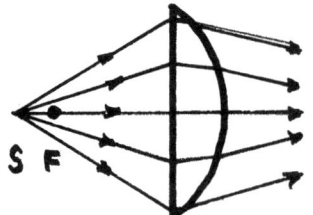 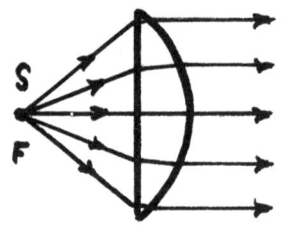 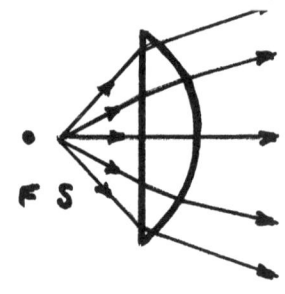

a

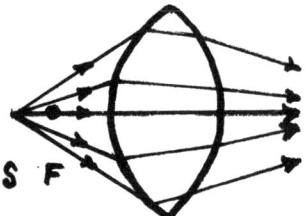 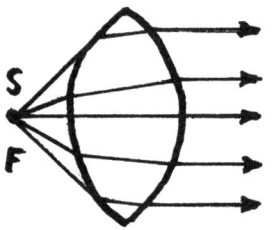 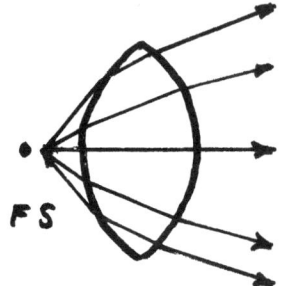

b

Figure 20

Two types of lens are used commonly on stage lighting instruments. They are called "plano-convex" lenses and "double-convex" lenses. Although their shapes differ slightly, as shown in Figure 20, they have similar effects on the light rays. If the lamp, or light source, is situated at the focal point of the lens, the refracted light will be beamed in parallel rays. If the lamp is between the focal point and the lens, the rays will bend outward, or spread. If the focal point is between the lamp and the lens, the rays will bend inward, or converge.

If you understood the above, you can easily see how the diameter of a light beam may be increased or decreased by moving the lamp closer to or farther from the lens. When you "focus" a light, actually all you are doing is changing the distance between the lamp and the lens. A better way of stating it would be to say that you are changing the position of the lamp in relation to the focal point of the lens.

Some lenses have closer focal points than others. This factor is governed by their diameter and thickness. The thicker the lens, the shorter the focal length. The advantage in using a thicker lens is that it is possible to get the lamp closer to the lens before you reach the focal point. The closer to the lens you can get the lamp, the stronger the light beam, because more of the rays of light are able to reach the lens. The disadvantage of this is that thicker lenses absorb more heat, and the probability of cracking is increased. Many lighting instruments will partly compensate for this by using two thinner lenses, each with a longer focal length, which when used together effect a total focal length that is equivalent to that of a thicker lens. This practice, in turn, increases the cost of the instrument.

In order to overcome these problems, a French physicist, Augustin Fresnel, developed a lens that is now known as the Fresnel lens (pronounced freh-nehl′). He devised a

Reflectors and Lenses / 35

Figure 21

lens with the curvature of a thick plano-convex lens, but used less glass. He did this by stepping back the curvature in ringlike steps as shown in Figure 21. You probably have noticed similar concentric rings on automobile headlights.

The Fresnel lens resolved the problems caused by the thicker lens, but created another circumstance. The only inexpensive way to make the lens is by use of a molding process that creates minor imperfections in the glass. That factor, plus the diverse angle on the outer face of the lens, causes the fresnel lens to throw a beam of diffused light rays. Therefore, you cannot get a sharp-edged beam of light from a Fresnel lens. On the other hand a diffused beam has certain advantages, as will be discussed in later chapters.

A more recent development is called the "step lens." This lens is made thinner by cutting the steps in the inner, or back, surface of the plano-convex lens, as shown in Figure 22. By using the step lens, it is possible to get a sharp-edged beam of light when you need it. Even then, however, the beam is not as clearly defined as the one resulting from the standard plano-convex or double-convex lens. You will not see many double-convex lenses today, because they tend to be even thicker than the plano-convex, and their characteristics are similar in all other respects.

This concludes the portion of the book that deals with the major components in a lighting instrument; namely, the source of light, the reflector, and the lens. In the next chapter we shall see how these devices are utilized to produce the various types of lighting instruments.

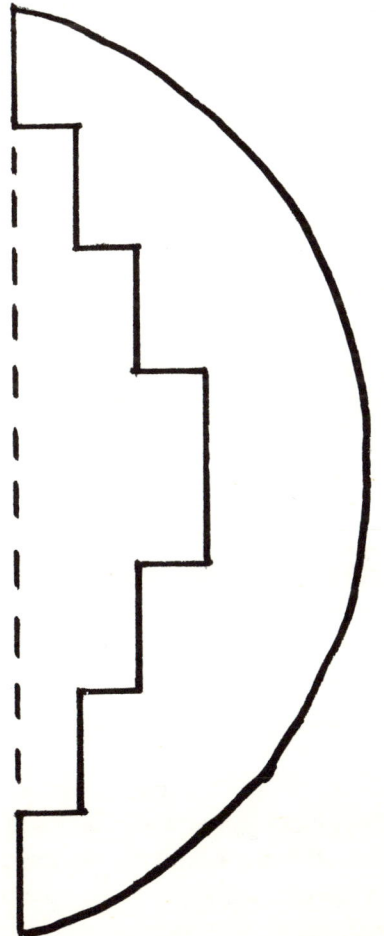

Figure 22

Chapter V

LIGHTING INSTRUMENTS

How would you determine the type of instruments you will need to light your stage? You might say, "I'm no expert. How would I know?" On the other hand you might remember what we discussed in Chapter I and apply it in the following analysis.

The major reason for using stage lights is for visibility. Other important purposes involve plausibility, mood, and composition. In order to obtain good visibility and emphasis lights with strong concentrated beams are needed. In order to enhance plausibility, create mood, and obtain good composition, one uses lights that are subtle, general, and wide-beamed.

Based upon this reasoning, we can classify our stage lights in four categories according to their use. One category covers lights used for specific area lighting; the second is for general lighting; the third covers tonal, or mood, lighting; and the final category takes care of special effects.

We obtain our specific area lighting with the use of spotlights. Floodlights are used for general area lighting, and floodlights and/or striplights for tonal lighting. You can create most special effects with either spotlights or special projectors.

One of the most exciting words in our stage lighting vocabulary is the word "spotlight." To the general public the term paints a vivid theatrical picture of a cone of light centered upon a dramatic performer, isolated like an island in a sea of darkness. To the actor and technician it describes a most necessary instrument for their success. It does more than create visibility. It magnifies, it emphasizes, it dramatizes. More than any other theatrical device, it can pick up a magnetic personality or a tense moment and carry it across the void into the hearts of the audience. A stage without spotlights is like a flashy sports car without wheels, or a stereo sound system without speakers. Just as you need a public address system to project sound over a great distance, you also need spotlights to project the visual aspects of the theatre.

The simplest, and original, spotlight is the box type shown in Figure 23. It contains a spherical reflector, a plano-convex lens, and a globular, medium-screw base lamp. As you can see, they are enclosed in a rectangular, metal box, which we shall call the casing. The lamp sizes are 250 and 500 watts, although you will find some of the larger box spots use 750- and 1,000-watt lamps.

In Figure 23 you can see a small knob on the top of the box. It is used to open and close the access door through which you can change lamps. This door is usually in one of three positions; either at the top, rear, or front of the instrument. The disadvantage of the rear door is that you will find it difficult to get at the lamp because the reflector obstructs your path. In fact, one manufacturer actually put a spotlight on the market a few years ago with a rear access door and insuf-

Lighting Instruments / 37

Figure 23

ficient clearance between the reflector and the casing to get the lamp through. It was necessary to dismantle the reflector in order to change lamps.

The top access door allows clear and easy access to the lamp. The only disadvantage occurs when the light is hung from the overhead and is all set and focused. In order to open the door, you usually have to turn the light downward. You will then have the task of resetting the light after changing the lamp.

Front-access spotlight doors actually hold the lens system and frame. The frame for the lens is hinged to the instrument casing. When you unlatch it, it will swing open, giving easy access to the lamp. Front-access

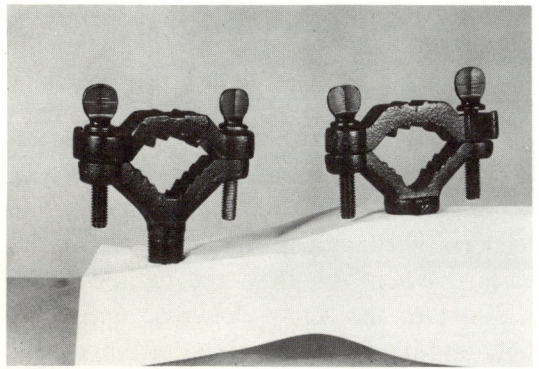

Figure 24

38 / **Practical Stage Lighting**

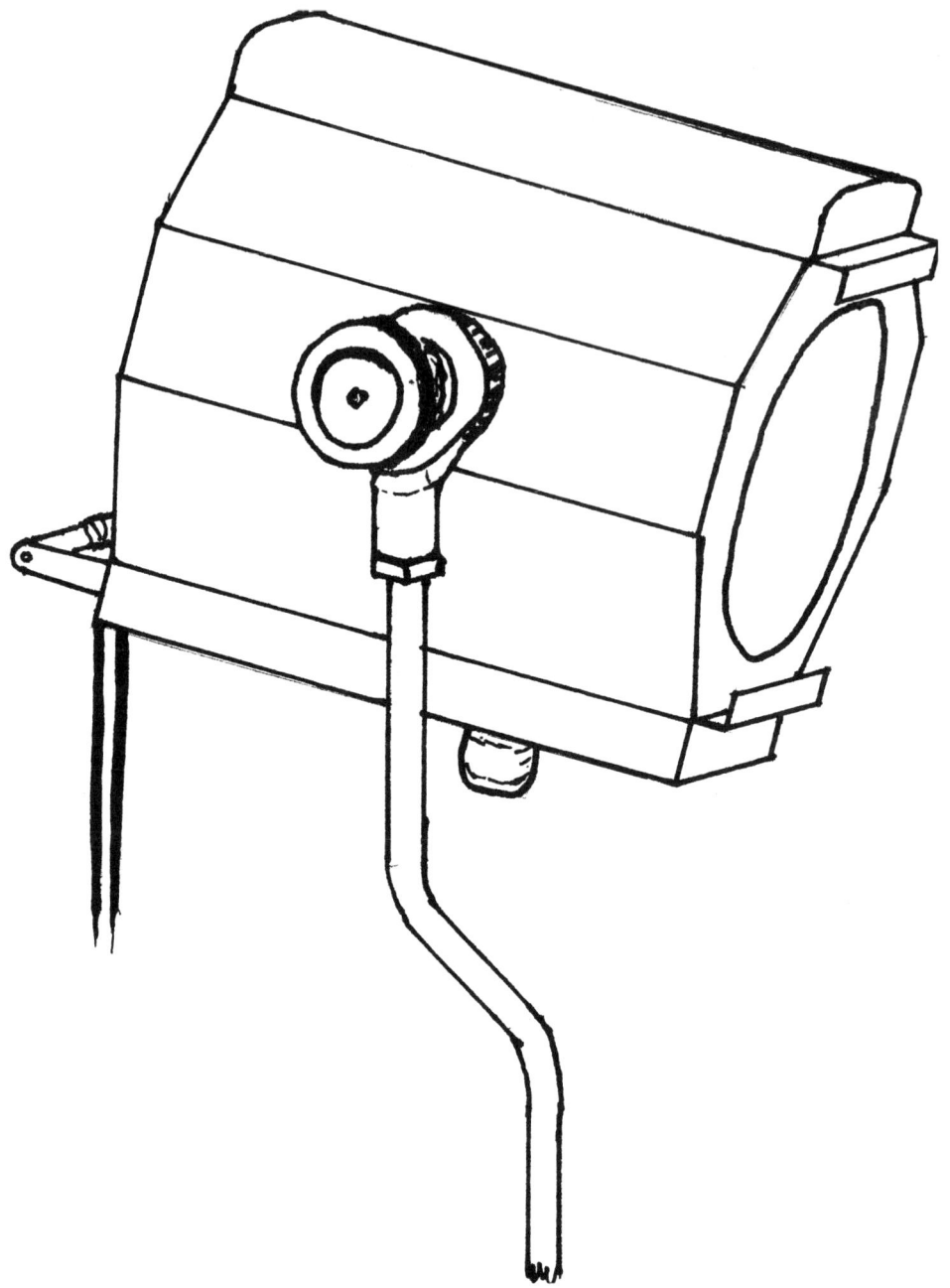

Figure 25

doors that swing sideways are better than those that swing up or down because the lenses are not as liable to fall out and break.

When you focus a spotlight your purpose is to increase or decrease the diameter of the beam of light. In the box-type spotlight you do this by sliding the lamp socket assembly closer to or farther from the lens. On the bottom of the casing you will find a thumbscrew or an insulated knob that is connected directly, through the casing, to the socket assembly. If you turn the screw, or knob, counterclockwise it will loosen and will slide back and forth in a slot on the bottom of the casing. When you have the desired beam width, turn the screw clockwise until it is tight and it will be locked in place until you wish to refocus the light.

Lighting Instruments / 39

On some lights the reflector is independent of the socket assembly and remains in a fixed position regardless of where you set the focus. The lighting instrument is more efficient, however, if the reflector and the lamp are kept the same distance apart. In better spotlights, therefore, the reflector will be part of the socket assembly and will move as the lamp moves. In that way the distance between them remains constant.

Since the wiring is connected, through the casing, directly to the socket, you must leave

Figure 26

Figure 27

enough slack in the pigtail so that the socket will slide freely to both ends of the slot without creating a strain on the wire.

You will find that two types of adjustment are used to direct, or set, your light on the desired object or stage area. One is for vertical movement and the other is for horizontal movement.

The adjustments used for vertical movement are the bolts on each side of the casing where the yoke is attached to the casing. These bolts differ on instruments of different

Lighting Instruments / 41

manufacture. Some are thumbscrews. Some have insulated knobs or small wheels. Many have hexagonal ⅝" bolt heads. By loosening the bolts on both sides of the instrument, you will free the instrument to swing on the yoke in a vertical arc. When it is in the desired position, you can tighten both bolts to lock it in place.

At the point where the top of the yoke is attached to the clamp, there is another bolt, which usually has a hexagonal ⅝" bolt head. Most C-clamps (see Figure 24) also

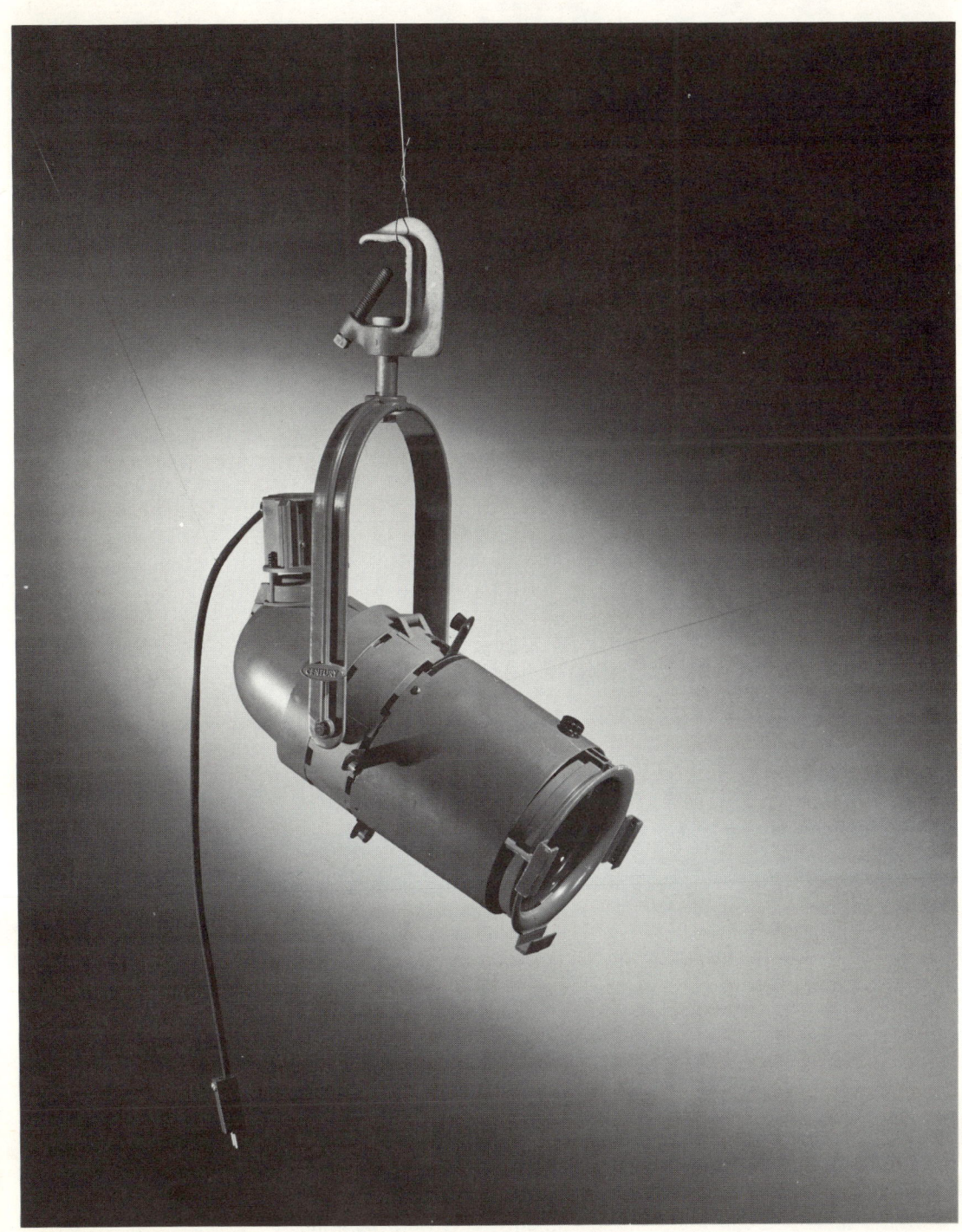

Figure 28

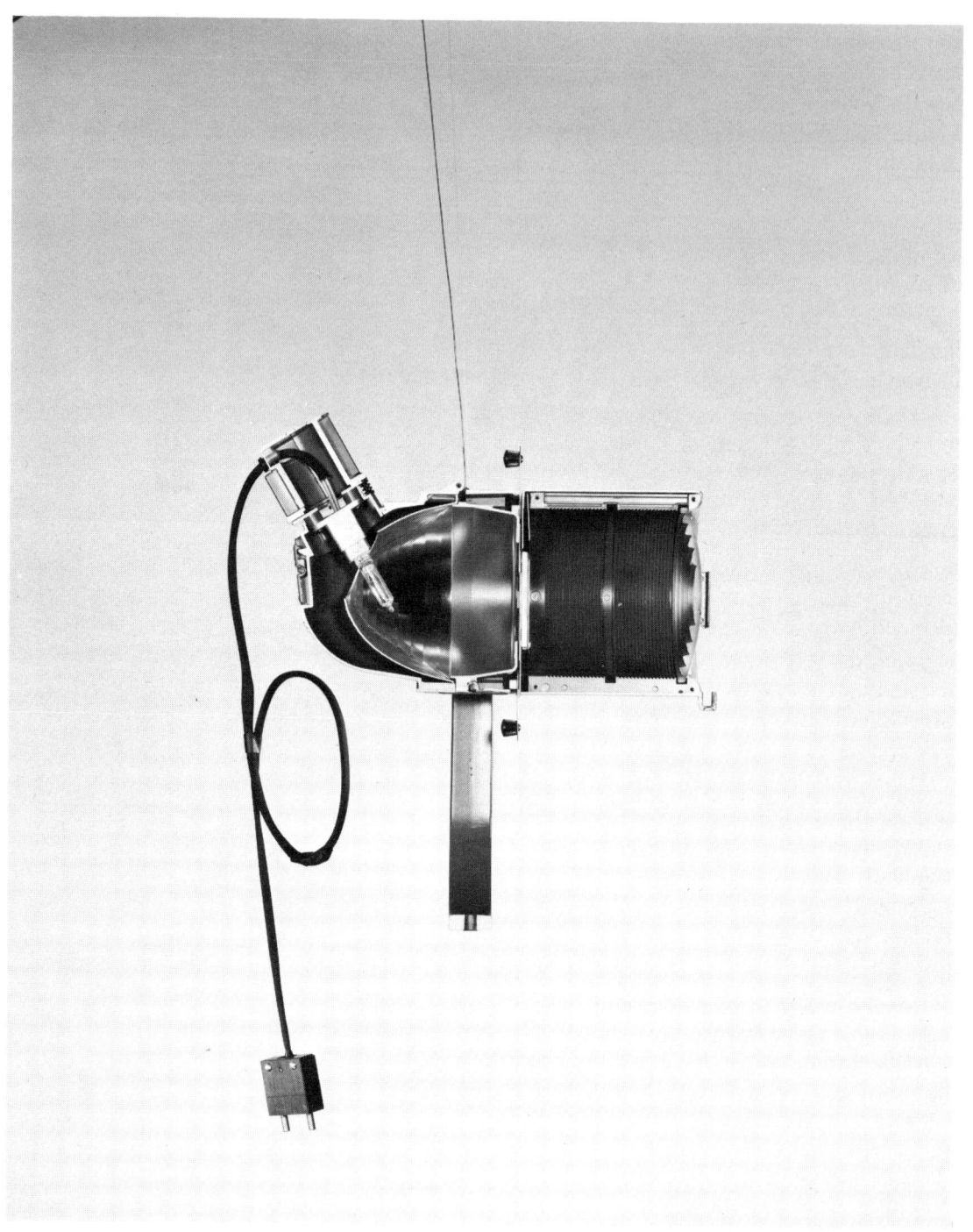

Figure 29

have a setscrew on the shaft with a rectangular ⅜″ bolt head. After loosening either of these bolts, you may swing the instrument on the clamp shaft in a horizontal arc. By tightening the bolt, you can lock the instrument in the desired horizontal position. If your clamp has both bolts, make sure they are both tightened when you wish to lock the instrument in position. You need loosen only one of them, however, to move the instrument horizontally.

Although some box-type spotlights are

larger than 500 watts, most of the larger spotlights have casings that are shaped similarly to hexagonal tubes, as in Figure 25. Some casings are cylindrical, as shown in Figure 26. The larger wattages, of course, require mogul-base lamps rather than the medium base. In all other respects their features and operation resemble the box-type spotlight.

Another variation of the box-type spotlight is the Fresnel spotlight. The outstanding feature is, of course, the fact that this instrument has a Fresnel lens. Figure 27 shows a typical Fresnel spotlight. Many models use tubular lamps with prefocus, or bayonet, bases. They may also be obtained with quartz lamp sockets. Again, their features and operation do not differ from the box-type spotlight. You can use them effectively to light an acting area that you wish to blend with its adjacent areas and whose edges need not be clearly defined. Most Fresnel spotlights have spherical reflectors of a larger diameter than is found in their box-type counterparts.

The ellipsoidal spotlight, shown in Figure 28, is so called because it features an ellipsoidal-shaped reflector. This instrument is frequently called a "Leko." The nickname is derived from the trade name "Lekolite" used by one of the manufacturers. Most ellipsoidal spotlights have cylindrical casings with ellipsoidal-shaped back ends.

Since the source of light must be set at the exact focal point of the ellipsoidal reflector, the position of the lamp is important. You will find that the lamp socket, therefore, is a prefocus, bayonet, or bipost style. Tubular-shaped lamp bulbs are used.

Notice in Figure 29 that the lamp is inside the reflector right at the focal point. You can easily remove the entire lamp assembly, including the socket and pigtail, when you need to change lamps. It is found on the top of the rear of the instrument. On most models you need only loosen one or two thumbscrews or a simple clamping bar.

Ellipsoidal spotlights also contain shutters, a feature normally found in follow spotlights. Figure 29 identifies the top and bottom shutters, but does not show the right and left shutters, one of which you may be able to identify in Figure 28. The shutters are pieces of metal with knobs on the end. When you push the knob in toward the center of the instrument as far as it will go, the metal will mask the half of the light beam affected on that side of the instrument. When you pull it out as far as it will go, it will not interfere with the beam at all. By using all four shutters, you can change the shape of the beam to a rectangle or square. You can also slide each knob in an arc around the perimeter of the casing. By doing this you will change the angle at which the shutter masks the light beam. In this manner, you can shape the beam into almost any four-sided configuration you wish. Or, if you prefer, you can flatten less than four sides and leave the normal curved edge of the beam on the remaining sides.

Since ellipsoidal spots use a double-lens system, the light beam coming out of the instrument is reversed. Because of this you must remember that the top shutter will mask the bottom of the beam, the right shutter will mask the left side of the beam, and vice versa. You will find that the shutters are most useful in masking light spill on the proscenium arch, the audience, and the scenery.

Because of the design of the ellipsoidal spotlight, it is important that the lamp and reflector remain fixed in the casing. Therefore, you cannot focus the light by moving the lamp assembly as you focus other spotlights. Instead, you vary the distance between the lamp and the lenses by moving the lens assembly. In Figure 28 you will see a knob on the casing near the front of the instrument. A slot in the casing accommodates this knob. You have to turn it counterclockwise to unlock it. Then you slide it backward or forward until you have the desired focus. It will lock in position by tightening it in a clockwise rotation.

Another feature you may obtain when you

buy a new ellipsoidal spotlight is called an "iris" and is usually also available on follow spots. An iris is a shutter that opens and closes concentrically, allowing you to obtain a circular beam of light of varying diameters. It is controlled by a knob in the center of the top, or bottom, of the casing. If you turn the knob clockwise, the iris will close. If you turn it in the opposite direction, the shutter will open.

All other adjustments on the ellipsoidal spotlight work in the same way as their counterparts on the box-type spot.

Consider, if you will, the various types and sizes of bolts, knobs, and adjustments on the many styles of lights. Multiply this by the number of manufacturers and their varying models. In order to work on them, a technician would have to carry a boxful of end wrenches up the ladder with him each time he adjusted a lighting instrument. It is in such instances that you will appreciate the value of the adjustable end wrench. Merely by turning the screw, you can adjust the tool to whatever size end wrench you may need.

In order to set a light properly, you will find that it is necessary to work on it while it is turned on. If the instrument is properly made, and if you observe the simple rules of safety set forth in Chapter II, the danger is minimal. An inconvenience, however, is that high-intensity incandescent instruments become very hot within a short period of time. To protect against burns, most technicians wear insulated gloves. It is recommended that you wear, if you are right-handed, a glove on your left hand with which you will handle the hot lighting instrument. This will leave the fingers of your right hand free to handle your tools and the small, insulated knobs properly. It is also advisable to wear a long-sleeved shirt to protect against arm burns caused by brushing against, and reaching around, the instrument.

In Chapter III, we mentioned the PAR lamp. It is designated PAR because the bulb has a parabolic shape. You have undoubtedly seen them. They are used frequently for outdoor lighting and window displays. They are similar in shape to sealed-beam automobile headlights. We mention the PAR lamp again in this chapter because it is, in itself, a lighting instrument. The conical, or parabolic, surface of the bulb is aluminum-coated causing it to become a parabolic reflector. The filament of course is the source of light, and the face, or disc-shaped portion, of the bulb may serve as a lens. Three types of face are found commonly on PAR lamps. The plano-convex and the Fresnel-type faces are used on PAR lamps intended for use as spotlights. Most PAR lamps are designed for use as floodlights, and the glass forming the face has parallel surfaces. In some cases the face on the floodlight will be stepped or ringed so as to further diffuse the light.

The PAR lamp has limited use as a spotlight because, even with a plano-convex lens, a great amount of light escapes, and the result is a broad beam of light with a highly concentrated smaller center beam. Where you can use diffused light beams, however, you will find that the PAR lamp is an inexpensive lighting instrument. You can obtain them in wattages ranging from 75 to 600

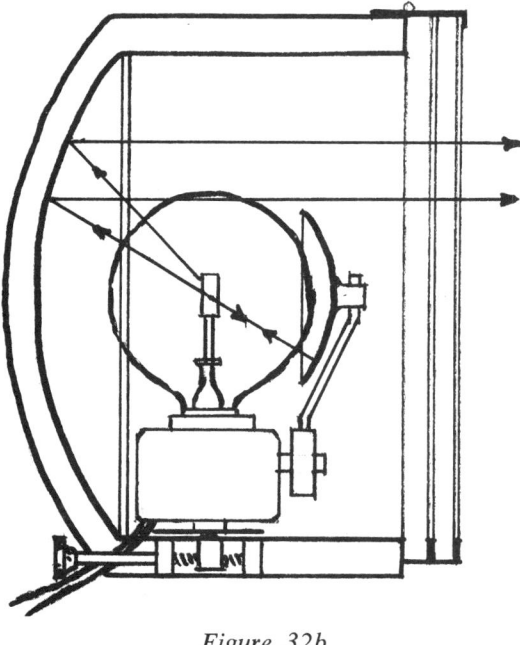

Figure 32b

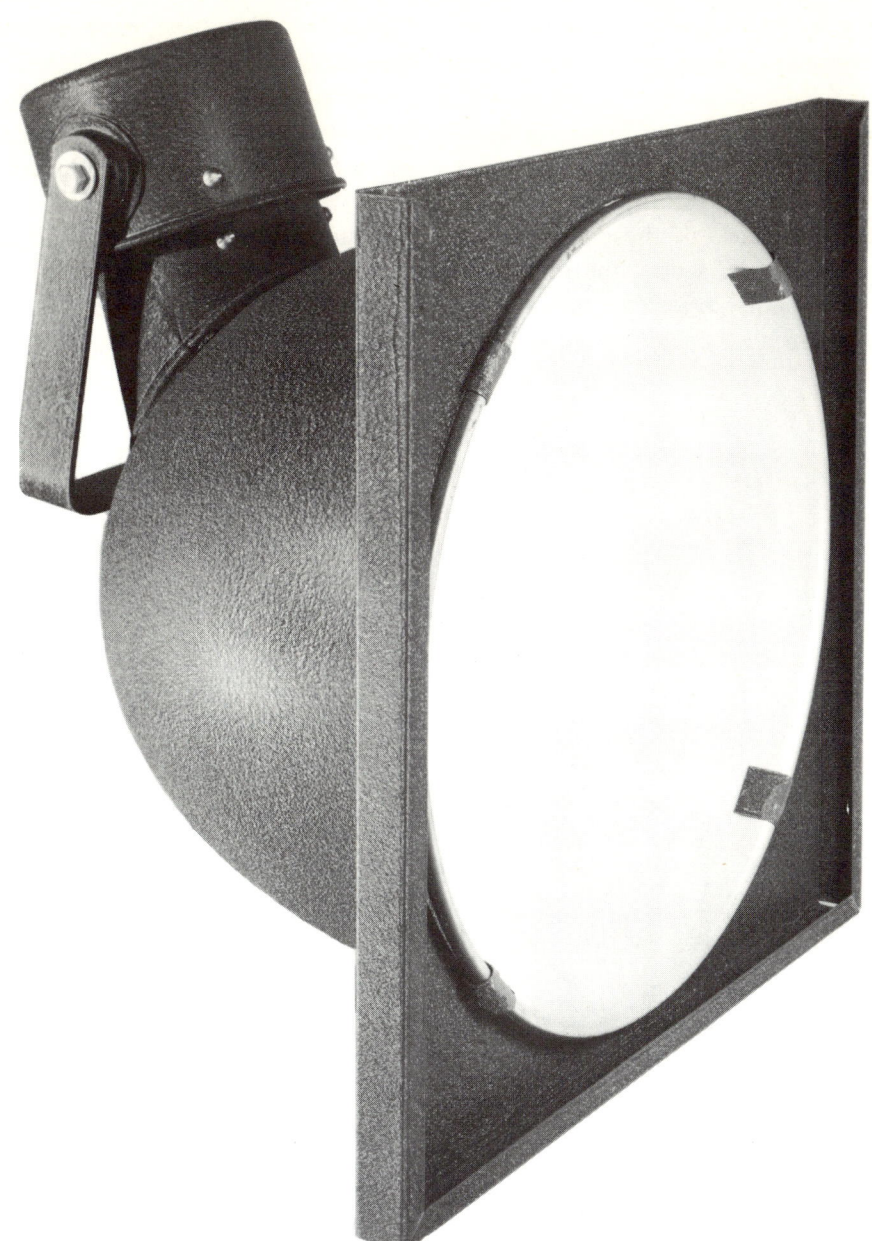

Figure 30

incandescent, and it is now possible to buy quartz PAR lamps that are 500 and 1,000 watts. When you buy 1,000-watt quartz PARs, inquire into the anticipated life span. Some are rated for the normal quartz life span of 4,000 hours; however, others are rated as low as 16 hours.

The structural differences between spotlights and floodlights is that the floodlights do not need lenses. Floodlights are categorized chiefly by the shape of their reflectors.

You will find that the ellipsoidal reflector floodlight, known commonly as a "scoop," is the most popular floodlight. It is shown in Figure 30. You can obtain it in sizes ranging from 75 watts to 2,000 watts. You may use scoops for cyclorama and backing lighting, general stage area lighting, window lighting, and tonal lighting. When you order scoops, also order color frames to accompany them;

otherwise you may be sent an instrument that does not have a slide to hold your color frame.

An olivette (see Figure 31) is a box-shaped floodlight, which may or may not have a built-in reflector of any shape. Its use has decreased because of the popularity of the scoop. Unlike the scoop, the olivette is not particularly suitable for cyclorama lighting. You can use it for backing lighting, general stage area lighting, window lighting, and tonal lighting.

The beam projector is a specialized floodlight. Figure 32 shows a beam projector. It uses a parabolic reflector to cast parallel rays of light and a spherical reflector in front of the lamp to recast the nonparallel beams coming directly from the lamp. It throws a beam of light that has as many of the characteristics of sunlight as can be reproduced

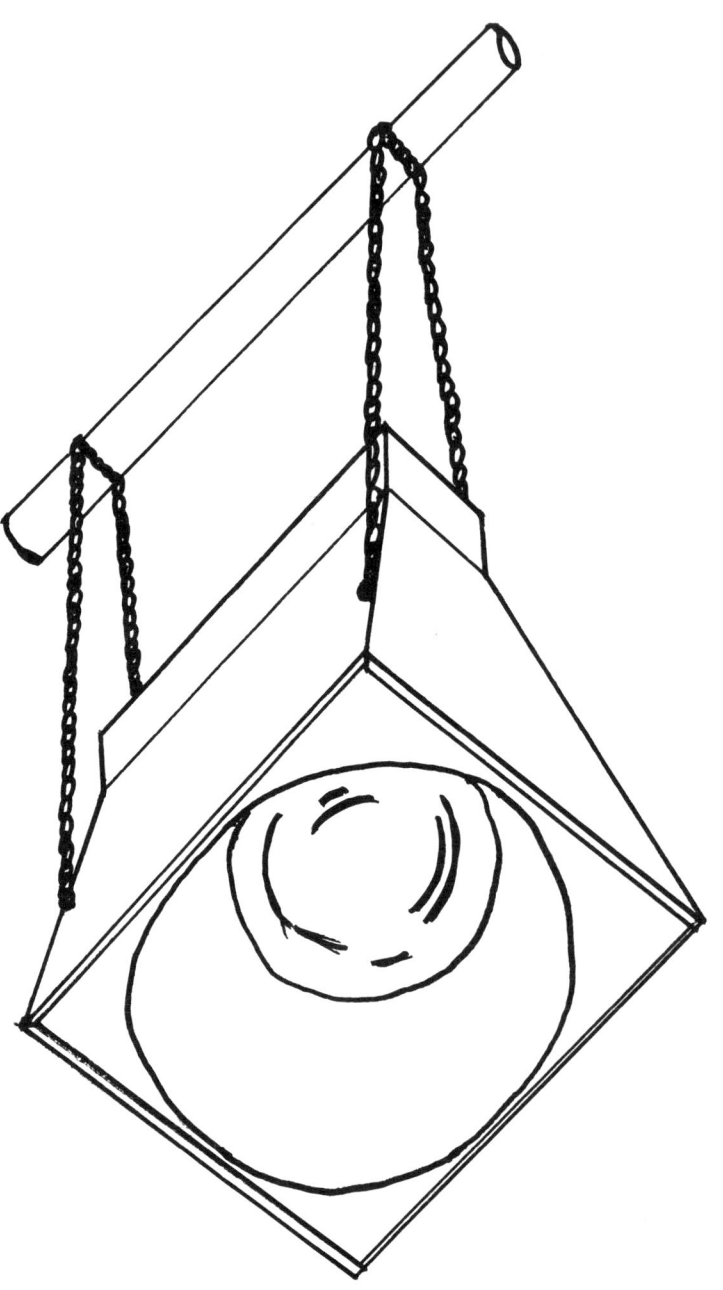

Figure 31

Lighting Instruments / 47

Figure 32a

artificially. You can obtain this instrument in wattages varying from 250 to 2,000. You may use it effectively as sunlight, moonlight, window lighting, side lighting, and back lighting.

Striplights are rows of sockets, for low-wattage lamps, placed in a troughlike casing as shown in Figure 33. The casing itself serves as a crude reflector. Some striplights provide an individual compartment for each light. The most modern have glass covers for each lamp compartment, as shown in Figure 34. The advantage of the glass covers is that you may use colored glass. On the other hand, colored lamp bulbs may be used. We will discuss this in more detail in Chapter XII.

A properly constructed striplight will contain three separate electrical circuits. Each circuit will control every third lamp. This is necessary so that you may control three colors individually if you desire.

When striplights are hung overhead, they are called border lights. When they are installed in the floor across the front of the stage, they are called footlights. When they are hung vertically on each side of the stage behind the curtain, they are called tormentor lights.

Most auditoriums have footlights and rows of border lights. They are for general lighting for concerts and lectures. Footlights today are used only for special effects because of the grotesque, unnatural light they throw. One may use border lights, tormentor lights, and/or footlights very subtly for tonal and mood lighting. The most effective use that one can make of striplights today is as cyclorama lights—from above, below, and/or the sides. They may also be used to light backings.

Many special-effects lights are types of projectors. The three types designed for theatrical use are stereopticons, sciopticons, and Linnebach projectors. "Stereopticon" is another name for the standard slide projector. The disadvantage in using a stereopticon is the noise made by the fan when the instrument is in use. Various accessories are available for stereopticons, such as motorized slide changers, continuous film strips, and motor-driven zoom lenses.

A sciopticon is an attachment that you can use with a spotlight. The spotlight should be 1,000 watts or greater and must have a plano-convex lens system. Figure 35 shows a sciopticon attached to a spotlight. This instrument is motorized and may be used to project moving lighting effects such as rain, snow, fire, flame, water, etc.

The Linnebach projector, as shown in Figure 36, was designed by a man of that name, for the specific purpose of projecting scenery. It is a large, boxlike instrument that you may set on the floor or hang overhead. The major advantage of the Linnebach is that you may place it relatively close to the screen and still project a much larger image than is possible with any other type of projector.

It is a simple instrument consisting of a very high-powered lamp, a wide-angle-spread box, and a large slide. It usually

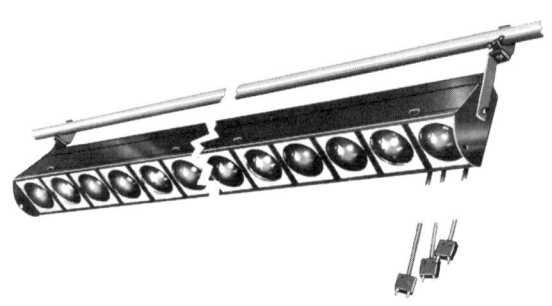

Figure 34

comes in two sizes—2,000 watts and 5,000 watts. The smaller instrument uses a slide that is approximately 1½′ square. The slide for the larger one is approximately 3′ square. The wide-angle spread between the small filament light source, which is close to the large slide, creates the large image within a short distance. On the other hand, it is impossible to obtain a clear, well-defined image, so the instrument is used chiefly for large massive figures and designs that do not depend upon detail.

You can make your own slides out of sheets of plate glass. Tape cutout silhouettes or colored transparencies to the glass to obtain the image you want. You will find that it is necessary to design the slides, by trial and error, on the stage because the sharp angle from the instrument to the screen causes great distortion for which you must compensate in the shape of the cutouts that you put on the slide. By using a scrim, or other translucent screen, you may project the image from behind if you wish. In doing so, be careful to conceal the projector from the audience; otherwise the powerful lamp will shine through the screen into the audience's eyes.

The use of projections of any kind presents a difficulty because the brightness of stage lighting usually washes out projected pictures. You will find it necessary to take all possible steps to keep reflected light rays, as well as direct rays, away from the projected surface.

Another special effect used on the stage is ultraviolet light. "Black light," as it is commonly called, is light whose rays are not vis-

Figure 33

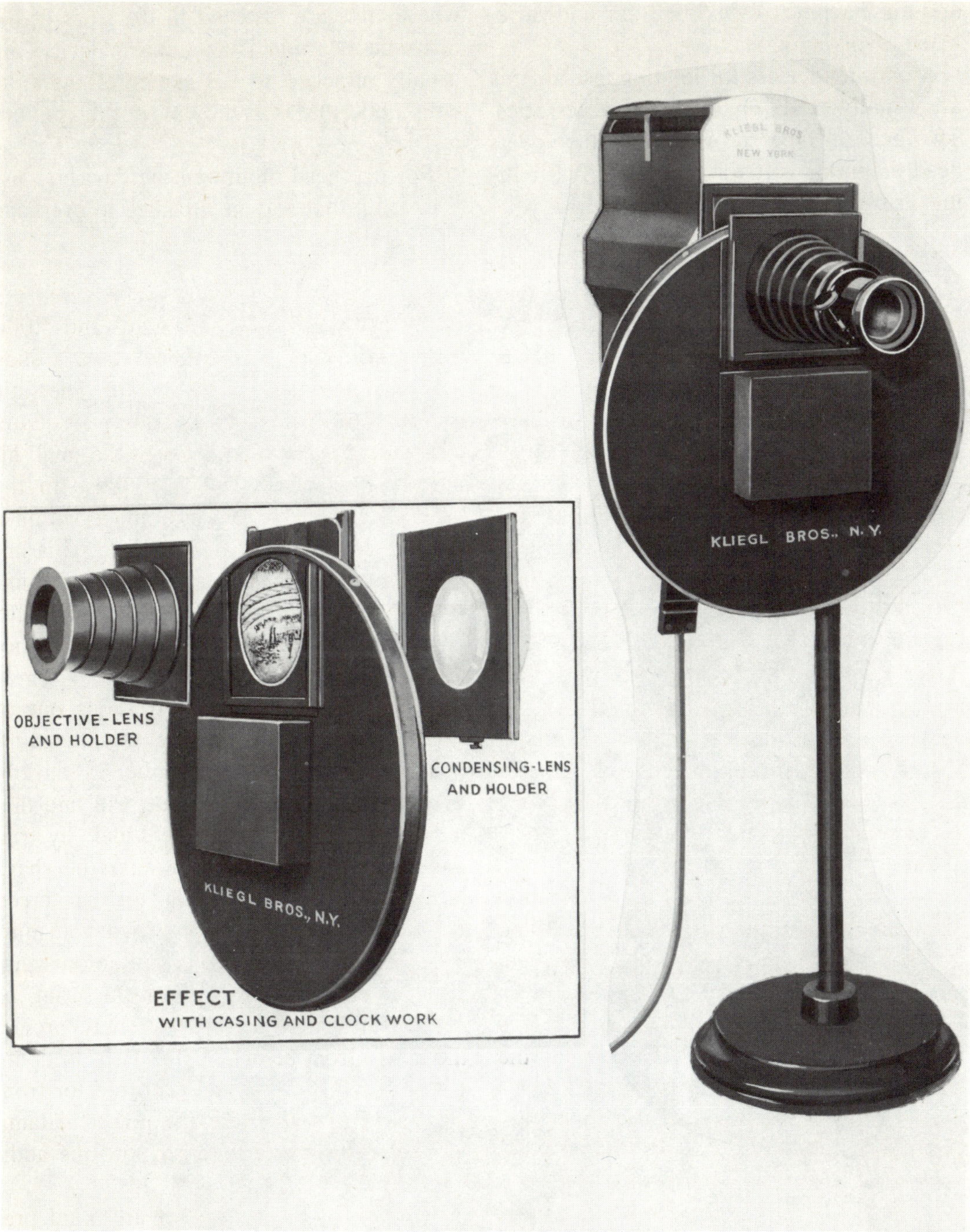

Figure 35

ible to the human eye until they have reflected from fluorescent paints, makeup, or materials. They usually produce an eerie effect. The effect cannot be seen unless all other lights are out. These instruments use mercury vapor lamps and ultraviolet filters. You can usually obtain them with a built-in transformer. If not, since they use direct current, you will have to use a transformer or battery in conjunction with the ultraviolet lights.

Other special effects that you may obtain from any theatrical lighting manufacturer include lightning devices, flash effects, smoke-

50 / Practical Stage Lighting

and-fog machines, twinkling stars, and variegated revolving lights.

Mounting devices for lighting instruments are usually sold separately as accessories. Two general types provide for either overhead mounting or floor mounting. All lighting instruments are furnished with a yoke whose ends are fastened to the sides of the instrument casing. The mounting devices are usually attached to the center of the yoke with a bolt that is usually part of the mounting device.

For overhead mounting the device to use is a clamp that may be attached to overhead

Figure 36

pipe battens. Two types of clamp are the most common. They are pipe clamps and C-clamps, as shown in Figure 24.

The pipe clamp is of two-piece construction that completely encircles a pipe. It has two bolts, or wing nuts, which connect the two pieces. When you tighten the bolts, the two pieces become clamped tightly in position around the pipe.

The C-clamp is the more popular device of the two, because it is easier to engage and disengage from the pipe. It can also be used on thick wooden battens. As the name implies, it is C-shaped and only partly encircles a pipe. A bolt is threaded through the lower end of the "C." When you tighten the bolt, it bites into the pipe, forcing it tightly into the pocket of the "C."

For floor mounting you can use various-size stands. The smallest is a mounting base that connects directly to the yoke and allows you to place the instrument on any flat surface. Screw holes in the base allow you to attach it firmly to a floor, table, wall, or ceiling, if you wish.

If you wish a higher mounting, you may use a pipe stand, as shown in Figure 37. It consists of a heavy metal base varying from 18″ to 30″ in diameter, a 1″ pipe that screws into the center of the base, a ½″ pipe that

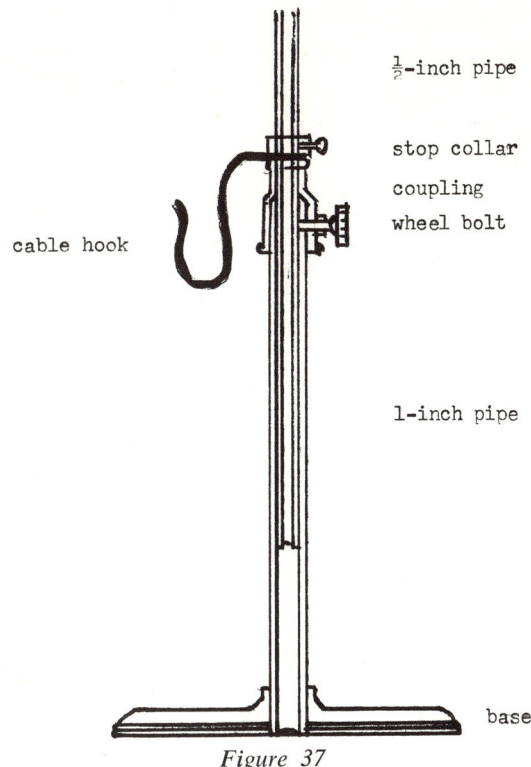
Figure 37

telescopes into the 1″ pipe, and a coupling with a stop collar and wheel bolt to tighten into each pipe.

Pipe stands come in two sizes. The small size telescopes from 4′ to 7′. The larger one extends from 5′ to 8′. Anything larger than those are specially designed and are usually

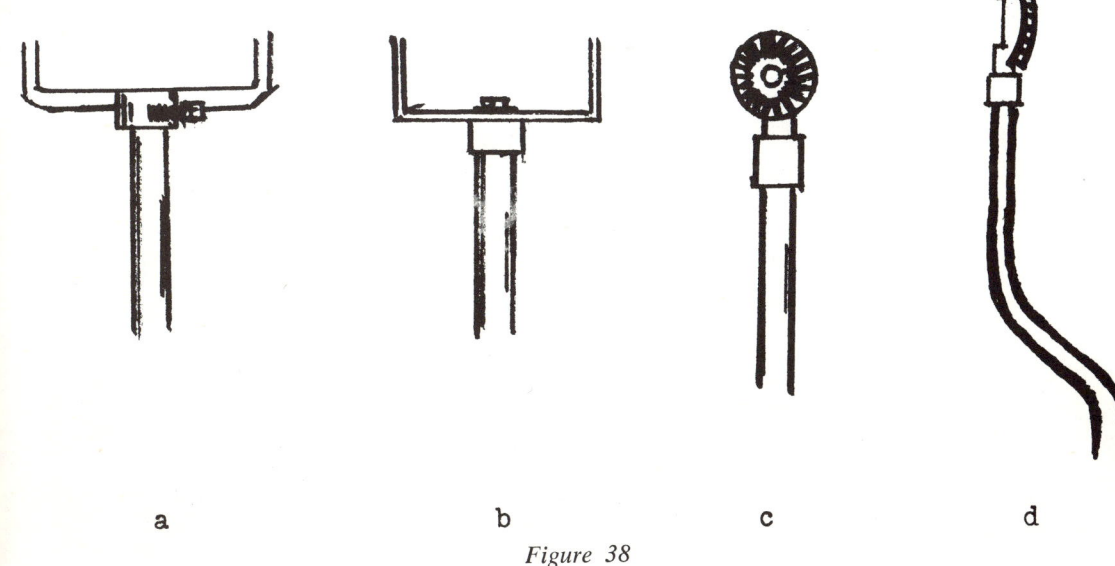
Figure 38

called light towers. The top of the ½" pipe has a fitting that you may connect directly to the yoke of the lighting instrument. If you prefer, however, you may use a rosette (see Figure 38), which attaches directly to the side of the instrument casing as shown in Figure 25.

Any spotlight may be installed upon a pipe stand and be used as a follow spotlight. When you order a follow spot from a manufacturer you get a high-wattage spotlight with shutters and/or an iris and long, insulated handles to control the instrument without danger of getting burned.

Before concluding this chapter on lighting instruments, we must make further mention of quartz lights. We have stated that lamps and socket conversion kits are available for use on standard lighting instruments. In addition, standard instruments are now on the market containing quartz lamp sockets. Some manufacturers who have specialized in quartz lights sell lighting instruments that differ from the standard stage lighting instruments. Those instruments have been designed for use in the motion picture, television, and photography industries.

An instrument is available, for instance, that may be focused from a broad-beamed floodlight to a highly concentrated spotlight. Like the PAR lamps, however, considerable "spill" occurs when it is used as a spotlight, and a well-defined beam is not possible.

By the same token, the floodlights cover wide ranges and are excellent for general lighting over a large area. Accessories called "barndoors" are available to confine the flooded area, but as in the case of the spotlights, there is spill and it is difficult to limit the light to a specific defined area.

Designs that correct those difficulties have resulted in quartz lighting instruments that do not differ greatly from standard theatrical instruments with quartz lamps. In conclusion, we can say that quartz lamps are excellent for stage use, but the lighting instruments in which they are used should not differ greatly from the best spotlights and floodlights that are designed specifically for theatrical use.

Chapter VI

CARE AND MAINTENANCE OF LIGHTING INSTRUMENTS

If you are in a typical theatrical group, organization or institution, you know as well as anyone that it is not easy to find funds for new lighting instruments. Therefore it is helpful, even necessary, to give tender, loving care to the instruments that you have been fortunate enough to obtain.

You will be handling your lights more when you set them than at any other time. The first step in setting a lighting instrument is to determine exactly where it is to be placed and to attach or clamp it firmly to that spot. If you use a mounting stand, make certain that the base is firmly attached to a solid object. Use screws that are strong enough to hold the weight of the instrument and stand. In most cases, you will clamp the instrument to a pipe batten. Make sure the clamp is firmly tightened to the batten. Do not risk damage to equipment or people by allowing an instrument to hang loosely at any time for any reason.

The second step is to plug the light in and turn it on to make sure it works. We will discuss shortly what you should do if it does not. Slide your color frame in, using the color that has been planned for that particular instrument. Loosen the horizontal and vertical adjustment bolts and you are ready to set the light.

To set the light, you first swing the instrument horizontally and/or vertically until it is aimed at the area or object that is to be lighted. Tighten the adjustments only enough so that the instrument will not move. Loosen the focusing adjustment and, using that adjustment, set the desired width of the beam. Tighten the focusing adjustment firmly. You may then find it necessary to loosen the horizontal and/or vertical bolts to make more exact adjustments in aiming the beam. Retighten those bolts firmly.

If the instrument has shutters, you should have opened them as wide as possible prior to setting the light. After focusing and re-setting, tighten the horizontal and vertical bolts only enough so that the instrument will not move. Then push the shutters in until you have shaped the beam as desired. Again, you may find it necessary to make final, exact adjustments in the vertical and/or horizontal setting. After that has been done, and both you and the directors are satisfied that the light is accomplishing its purpose, you may tighten all remaining adjustments so as to lock the instrument firmly in place.

Perhaps the second most frequent handling of lighting instruments will occur when you carry or transport them. Whether you carry a light across the stage or across the country, it is wise to protect the filament in the lamp from sudden shock as a result of banging the instrument into another object. It happens most frequently when carrying an instrument up a ladder. If you loosen both the vertical and horizontal adjustments,

54 / Practical Stage Lighting

the instrument will tend to move with the collision and absorb some of the shock. It is still necessary for you to be careful to avoid banging it because the filament may still break, and the lenses, too, are fragile.

If it is necessary to transport instruments by truck to another building, additional precautions should be taken. First of all, remove all lamps and pack them carefully in compartmented containers and/or well wrapped in paper. If possible, transport the lamps by automobile or in the cab of the truck.

If the lighting instruments are carried in containers, use wooden boxes or steamer trunks and pack them carefully so they won't move, rattle, or shift position. You may loosen the horizontal and vertical adjustments to make it easier to pack them. Try to keep the clamps and other protruding objects away from the lenses of adjacent instruments. Make sure that the lid of the container is tightly closed and well fastened.

It is also possible to transport lighting equipment unpacked. In such cases, a batten must be securely installed in the truck and you must clamp the lights securely to the batten. Again, the lamps should be removed and packed separately. You should also loosen the vertical and horizontal adjustments to lessen the shock of each bump and jar of the truck. This helps to protect the lenses. Make sure that all objects and adjacent instruments cannot accidentally bump into any of the lenses.

Lamps are expensive, and each minute of their life span should be conserved. Lighting instruments should be lighted only during actual performances, dress and technical rehearsals, and setting, adjusting, and checking periods. At all other times use "worklights" that contain less expensive lamps.

What do you do when an instrument doesn't work? The following is a good checklist that you should follow in the order listed:

1. Make sure all switches are on.
2. Make sure the dimmer controls are in the "full-up" position.
3. Make sure all cable connections are tight.
4. Check the shutters to see that they are not closed.
5. Replace the fuse or check the breaker switch position.*
6. Replace the lamp.

It may not be possible to do some of the above tasks during a performance. Check whatever you can and let the rest wait until you have a proper opportunity. Of course, when you have found the trouble, there is no need to continue through the checklist.

Insofar as general routine care of lighting instruments is concerned, the biggest problems are dust and rust. An accumulation of dust in certain places can greatly reduce the candlepower of a lighting instrument. Rust in some places can have the same effect, but in other places it has an effect upon your ability to adjust and set your lights.

You should establish the practice of checking and cleaning each instrument before each production. Remove all dust, of course, but make sure that the reflector, lamp bulb, and lenses are clean. An air gun is suitable for removing dust from all cracks and corners, but you should use a soft cloth (cheesecloth is excellent) to remove dust from the reflector, lamp bulb, and lenses.

If the instrument has a multilens system, make sure you clean both surfaces of each lens. They are usually held in place by a tension ring that fits in a groove in the casing around the perimeter of the lens. You can remove the ring by squeezing the angled ends of the ring together with a pair of pliers. The lens will fall out when you remove the ring. Be careful not to let the lens fall and break. Before removing a lens, you should make note of which side of the lens faces in and which faces out, so you can replace it in the correct position after you

---

* If a fuse is burned or the breaker switch is tripped, make sure you know what has caused it and have the condition corrected before you replace the fuse or reset the breaker.

Care and Maintenance of Lighting Instruments / 55

clean it. Water and, if necessary, soap may be used to remove any spots. Make sure all soap is rinsed off and the surfaces are completely dry before replacing the lens.

Rust is a problem on most metallic surfaces of the instrument. If it forms on the inner surface of the reflector, you will need a new reflector. Usually, however, it is plated with a rustproof coating. The largest problem that rust can cause is on the bolts, screws, and adjustments. If they are allowed to rust, they will become very difficult, if not impossible, to turn. When there is any sign of rust in these areas, unscrew the bolt or adjustment as far as it will go. Then apply machine oil to the threads of the bolt and, if accessible, the threads of the socket it screws into. Work the bolt or adjustment back and forth, add more oil as necessary, and continue the procedure until it works easily to its tightest position as well as to its full open position.

Do not try to hammer a threaded device. If it is locked tight, apply penetrating oil to its exposed surfaces until it can be turned. If that does not work, you have allowed the rust to accumulate for too long, and the bolt must be drilled out with a power drill, and the hole rethreaded to take a new bolt.

Thumbscrews, handwheels, wing nuts, knobs, etc. are designed to be turned by hand. If you find it necessary to use a tool to turn them, do so very gently as too much force will break them. It is preferable to apply oil immediately and operate them by hand. In any case, apply oil as soon as possible, because that is the proper remedy for the condition.

When using oil, take special care not to get oil on any electrical wire or connections, since it is a conductor. Do not allow oil to get on insulation because it penetrates the insulation and decreases its insulating capability. It also causes rubber to dry, crack, and break. At the same time, remember that water is also a conductor as well as a rusting agent on metal. So keep your instruments completely dry. If you find it necessary to clean any materials that conduct electricity, the best cleansing agent to use is carbon tetrachloride, which may be obtained in electrical supply stores or most hardware stores.

Keep all lighting cables neatly coiled. Knots, kinks, and sharp bends tend to wear and break the insulation. Sometimes they even cause the wire inside the insulation to break. Even when in use, excess lengths of cables should be neatly coiled in an out-of-the-way area, or hung on a hanger on the wall.

When not in use, your lighting instruments should be stored in a dry, relatively dust-free area. Hang them on pipe battens, where they will be out of the way and not liable to be hit by other objects. If you have no such area available, it is better to leave them on their battens onstage than to try to store them in an unsuitable manner or area.

Chapter VII

BUDGET LIGHTING

We started the previous chapter by mentioning the financial problems that most theatrical groups encounter. Because of those problems, we stated, it is necessary to care for and preserve the equipment that we can afford to own. It may have occurred to you, when reading those statements, that it is somewhat difficult to maintain equipment if you can't afford to buy any to begin with. This chapter, therefore, deals with some of the practices you may use to obtain adequate lighting effects without spending much money.

The problem may be approached in two ways, and it is recommended that you use both, letting your pocketbook be your guide. One approach is to find bargains in manufactured equipment, and the other is to build your own. This subject matter is also divided into two areas: lighting instruments and lighting controls. In this chapter we shall discuss instruments and in Chapter XI we shall talk about budget lighting controls.

Looking for bargains is a continual process. It involves several things that you can do. Get your name on the mailing lists of all stage lighting manufacturers and theatrical supply houses. You may subject yourself to a lot of "junk" mail, but they will also advise you of special sales and bargains. A few months ago we bought brand-new 500-watt Fresnels at less than $20 each from a theatrical supplier on a special sale. They normally cost $25 to $30 at market prices in effect at the time of purchase.

Greater bargains than that may be realized by purchasing secondhand equipment. Watch the papers and magazines for theatrical groups going out of business and old theatres being torn down. You now know enough about lighting instruments to be able to determine the value of secondhand equipment. Look out for rust and check operability. A knowledgeable technician can get the best bargains in this manner. Don't be afraid to bargain, but remember that you may be competing with other bidders. Try to find out first.

Suppose no bargain sales are going on and you don't have time to wait for one. You can't afford even $20 per instrument. Theatrical groups and theatres going out of business are scarce, or nonexistent, in your area. You still need lighting instruments. What do you do?

That is when we take up the approach of building your own equipment. First, however, listen to words of warning. Many local ordinances, building codes, boards of directors, and/or school administrators frown upon homemade equipment for safety reasons. All practices recommended herein will result in safe equipment if you follow the directions and use the materials specified.

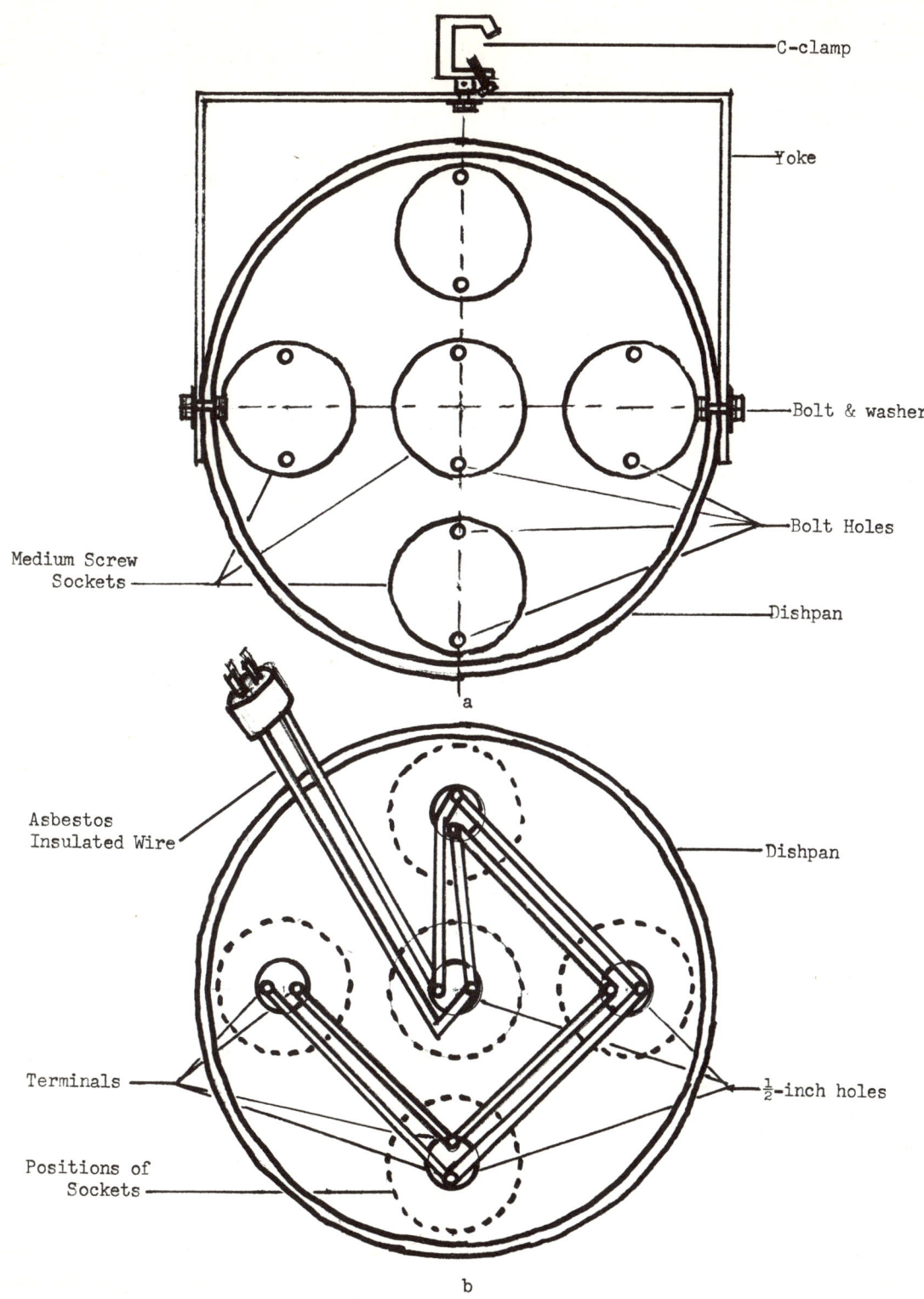

Figure 39

58 / Practical Stage Lighting

You must also continue to follow the safety precautions discussed in Chapter II.

One of the most common practices is the use of PAR lamps in swivel sockets that can be mounted on walls, ceilings, or wooden battens. It is even possible to buy, or make, color frames that attach to the socket or clip onto the lamp itself. These constitute satisfactory floodlights, but considerable light leakage will occur that cannot be controlled, so they are less satisfactory as spotlights unless you devise a method of containing the light spill.

An effective floodlight can be made out of a circular-shaped galvanized dishpan or washtub. You can bolt or weld one to five sockets to the bottom of the pan on the inside as diagrammed in Figure 39. Wire them as shown with asbestos-insulated wire. Run the wire on the outside of the pan. Drill holes through the bottom at each socket for the wire. Each hole drilled in the pan for the wire must have a rubber grommet to insulate the pan. The wire should also have a ceramic shield at that point to keep the metal from cutting into the asbestos insulation.

Shape a yoke out of strap iron with holes drilled on each end and in the center. Drill two holes opposite each other through the sides of the pan and bolt the yoke to the pan at those points. You may attach a clamp or other mounting device to the center of the yoke.

You can use various-sized pans, and the number of lamp sockets may be varied to increase or decrease the amount of light. Keep track of the total wattage of the lamps so that you do not overload the circuit. Small pans may be used in the same way with a single lamp as makeshift scoops. You will find that PAR lamps, globular lamps, or PS lamps are suitable. If the pan is not galvanized, it may not have a good reflecting surface. In such cases, line the inside of the pan with aluminum foil.

You can make striplights as shown in Figure 40 by covering one side of a 1″ x 6″ board with metal or, lacking that, aluminum foil. Then attach a row of lamp sockets in multiples of three, and wire each third socket together. The sockets should be spaced 6″ apart on center. Once again, use asbestos-insulated wire. Make a trough shape, as illustrated, by attaching a metal or wire frame, 6″ high, to one side of the board and a similar frame, 2″ high, to the other side of the board. Cover both frames with aluminum foil. Use 60-watt, colored A lamps in the

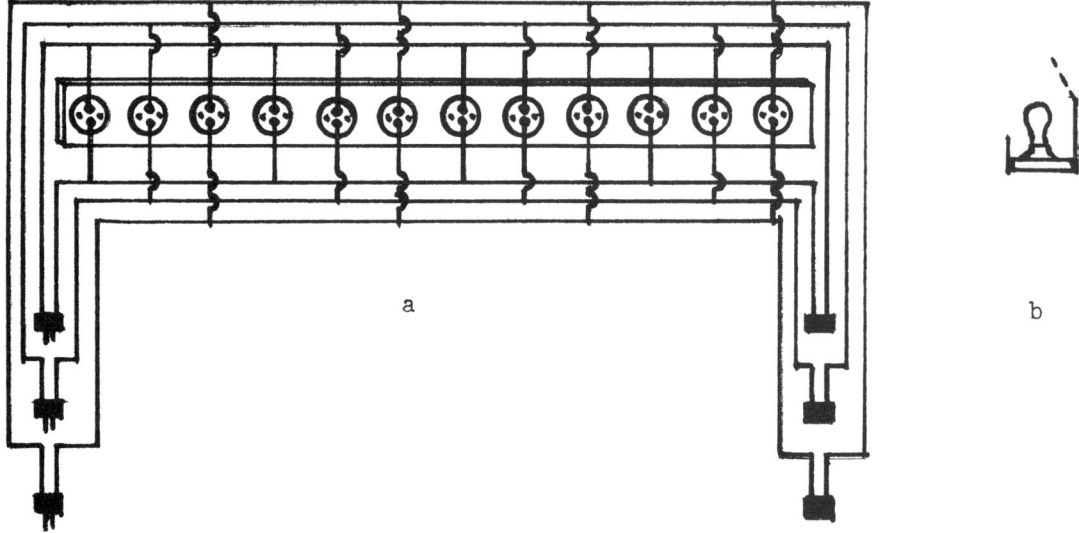

Figure 40

Budget Lighting / 59

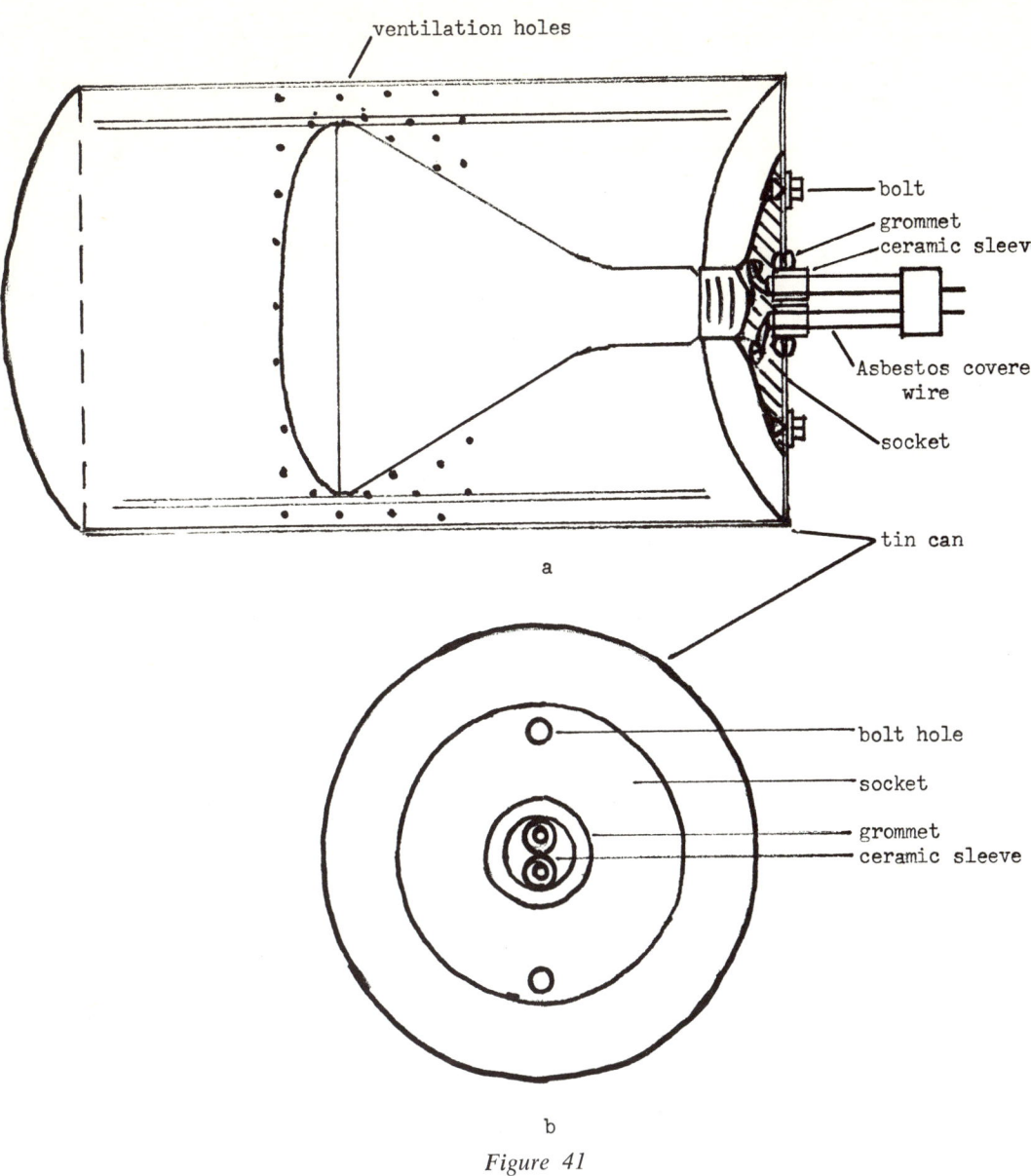

Figure 41

sockets. One circuit should have lamps with red bulbs, one with green, one with blue. A 6′-long striplight will contain twelve sockets, or three circuits of 240 watts each. If you make them any longer, they may become unwieldy because of their length and weight.

Lamps with dipped, or natural, colored bulbs may be ordered from most theatrical supply houses. They are usually P, S, or A shaped, any of which are suitable.

Spotlights have been made from stovepipe, lard cans, coffee cans, paint cans, etc. Of these, stovepipe is the least desirable because its inner surface is not reflective. In addition, it is not as common an item as it was in the 1930's and early 1940's. In selecting a can to use, look for one that is approximately 6″ or more in diameter. Most PAR lamps will fit inside a can of that size. Ascertain that the inside has an aluminum-colored surface, rather than a copper-colored one, for better reflectivity.

First, remove one end of the can with an automatic can opener to get a smooth, clean-cut opening. Then, cut a ⅜″ hole in the center of the other end, through which you

60 / **Practical Stage Lighting**

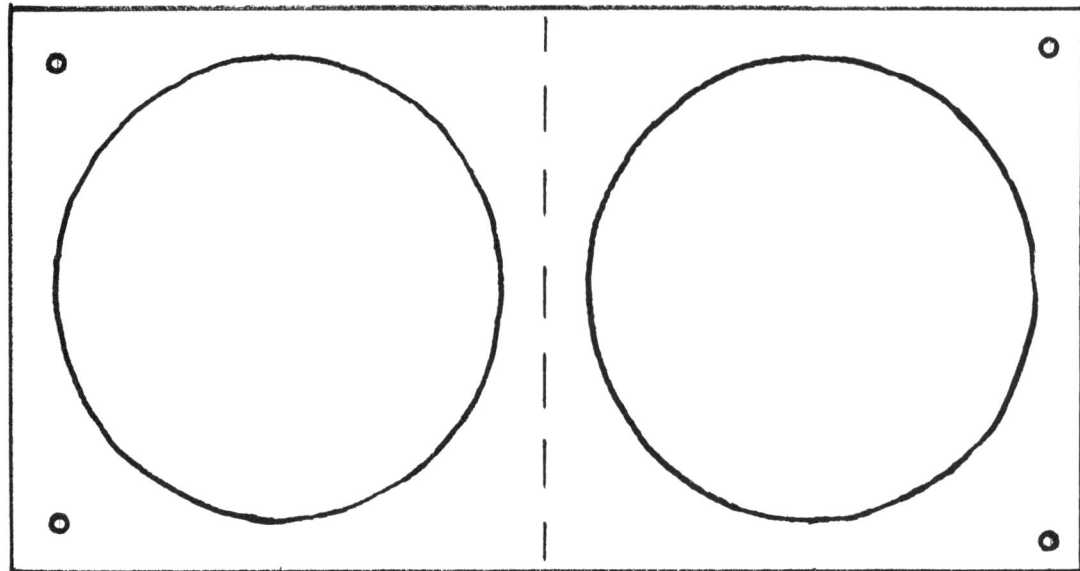

Figure 42

will insert the asbestos-insulated wire leads. A rubber grommet and ceramic shielding around each lead are recommended for that hole. Install the socket by bolting it to the inside of the closed end of the can. You will find it necessary to connect the wires to the socket before bolting the socket in place. Refer to Figure 41.

Using a sharp-pointed tool, punch holes in the sides of the can for ventilation. Try not to change the cylindrical shape of the can when you punch the holes. They should be about 1″ apart and should circle the can in at least a 3″ band in the area opposite the location of the filament of the lamp.

Although any type and size of lamp may be used, the spotlight will not be too effective unless the filament of the lamp is within the lower half of the can (the half closest to the socket). You should control this factor by comparing the length of the lamp you choose to the length of the can you select.

If you use PAR lamps, you will have a more efficient spotlight because they contain a built-in lens. In fact, if you use PAR lamps as spotlights on swivel sockets, you can cut down the light spill by covering them with a can. In such a case, cut a hole in the closed end of the can so that it will fit tightly on, or around, the socket assembly. You should use a rubber grommet to get a tighter fit and, even more important, to insulate the can from any possible contact with the electrical circuit. Don't forget to punch ventilating holes in the can.

Probably the peskiest problem with homemade spotlights and floodlights is the means of attaching color frames. Clip-on frames are sold for PAR lamps, but they usually use colored glass and are, therefore, expensive (more about this in Chapter XII). The heat from the lamp frequently burns gelatin color media on homemade lights. Plastic color media are probably the best inexpensive material to use.

It is recommended that you weld pieces of metal to the perimeter of the open end of the can. Use a standard color frame as a pattern to get the correct size, and shape the metal like a slide so the color frame may be easily inserted and removed. It is best to place the grooves on the bottom and two sides so that the frame will be held in place by the force of gravity. Grooves on the top and bottom alone do not always keep the frame from falling out at the wrong times.

If you do not have means of welding the metal, it may be bolted on, or you may be able to shape a usable frame holder out of a length of rigid wire such as a wire coat hanger. In such cases, it may be difficult to get a firm, sturdy connection, but if it holds the color medium in front of the light beam without the possibility of falling off, it will serve its purpose. Do not allow a loose color frame to hang over the heads of the audience, or where the actors and backstage personnel may bump into it and jar it loose.

In most cases you will find it less expensive to buy accessories than to build them. Two accessories that can be homemade rather easily, however, are color frames and substitutes for clamps.

Figure 42 shows the pattern for a homemade color frame. The various dimensions are not shown because they will vary according to the size and shape of the light. After cutting a pattern of the correct size out of a thin-gauge, soft sheet metal, bend it in half so that the holes coincide; insert the color medium between the two halves; then, using brass fasteners through the small holes in the corners, secure the open ends together.

You may use pipe fittings in place of clamps. Use a tee large enough to fit loosely around your pipe battens and pipe stand shafts. The tee's nominal size should be ¼" larger than the size of the pipe. Drill a ³⁄₁₆" hole in the wall of the tee and thread the hole with a ¼" x 20 t.p.i. (turns per inch) tap. This hole will then accommodate a ¼" thumbscrew as shown in Figure 43. The batten will fit through the arms of the tee, which can be secured by tightening the thumbscrew. You will probably find it necessary to use a reducing bushing in the outlet of the tee as shown in Figure 43, in order to adapt it for a piece of ½" pipe. If you're lucky, though, you may find a plumbing supplier who has the size tee you need with a ½" outlet. The ½" pipe should be 4" to 6" long. One end of this is screwed into the tee's outlet and the other end is bolted to the center of the yoke on the lighting instrument. You may then use the tee in the same way that you would use a clamp. You can still make your horizontal adjustments at the center of the yoke.

The disadvantage of using this is that it is necessary to unfasten your pipe batten at the ends in order to slide the tees onto it. If you use tees, it is recommended that you leave a sufficient number of them on your pipe battens permanently and, as you use them, slide them to the desired location and connect your lighting instrument to them.

The preceding suggestions are inexpensive, yet safe, ways of building lighting equipment. Do not let them limit your creativity. If you have materials and facilities to build more sophisticated equipment, do so. Perhaps you can use reflectors or lenses. You may know of a metal-working shop that can shape casings. By all means, build the best equipment you can afford, but don't spend more money building it than it would cost to buy it.

As important as safety is, it is even more important when using makeshift equipment. Make sure that all mechanical connections

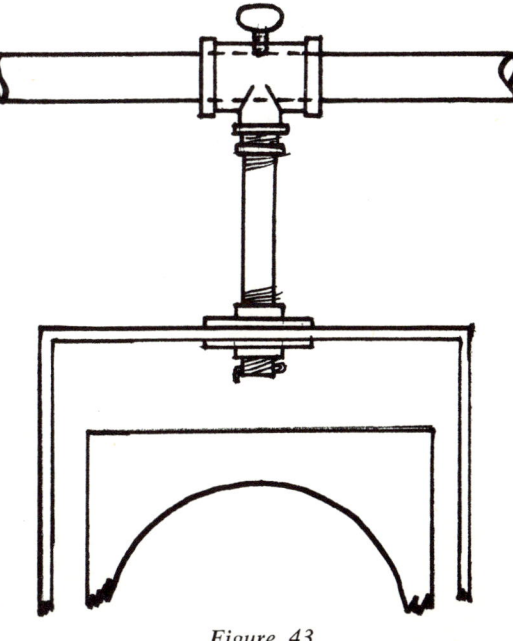

Figure 43

are secure. Make sure that all circuits are well insulated, and protect the insulation against damage from friction, sharp edges, or any other deteriorating conditions. Use only heat-resistant materials. Remember that all electrical connections must make good tight contact to one another—they must be electrically sound, physically secure, and well insulated.

Chapter VIII

DIMMERS—RESISTANCE AND AUTO-TRANSFORMER

In discussing lighting instruments we learned how you can control the size, shape, and direction of the light beam by using devices and accessories that are part of the lighting instruments. You can also control other qualities of the light beam. One of these is called intensity or candlepower. It is the brilliance or brightness of the light beam. You determine the highest, or maximum, intensity by the size of the lamp in the lighting instrument. The lowest, or minimum, intensity is always total darkness, which is properly controlled by the switch that disconnects the electrical current or, to use common terminology, turns off the light.

On the stage, however, you will find it necessary to use intensities that are at various points between the maximum and the minimum of any particular lighting instrument. In addition, in the course of a theatrical production, you will find it necessary to vary that intensity without access to the instrument. In many cases you will have to change it without turning off the light. Devices used to accomplish these tasks are called "dimmers."

The several types of dimmers can be classified into four general groups; resistance dimmers, auto-transformer dimmers, reactance dimmers, and electronic tube dimmers. The first two types are electrical devices and we will deal with them in this chapter. The latter two types pertain to electronic developments and will be discussed in the following chapter.

In principle, dimmers can be compared to water faucets or valves. When you turn on the faucet in your sink as far as it will go, the water comes rushing out at the greatest possible force that the pressure and system of pipes will allow. As you slowly close the faucet, the force and amount of water slowly diminish until the faucet is closed completely and the stream of water stops. When you operate a dimmer, you are controlling the electrical current just as the faucet controls the current of water. If you leave a dimmer in an intermediate position you will allow the current to flow through at a certain reduced, but steady, rate just as the water flows through a faucet that has been left partly open.

Since electricity flows through solid metal, whereas water flows through a hollow tube, the methods of decreasing the flow of electricity are different from the method of decreasing the flow of water. To understand this, we must again consider the electrical characteristics of materials. You should remember, by now, the difference between conductors and insulators. Remember, also, when we discussed filaments, we learned that some metals offer considerable resistance to an electrical current, whereas our best conductors offer very little resistance.

It is an established fact that you can

64 / **Practical Stage Lighting**

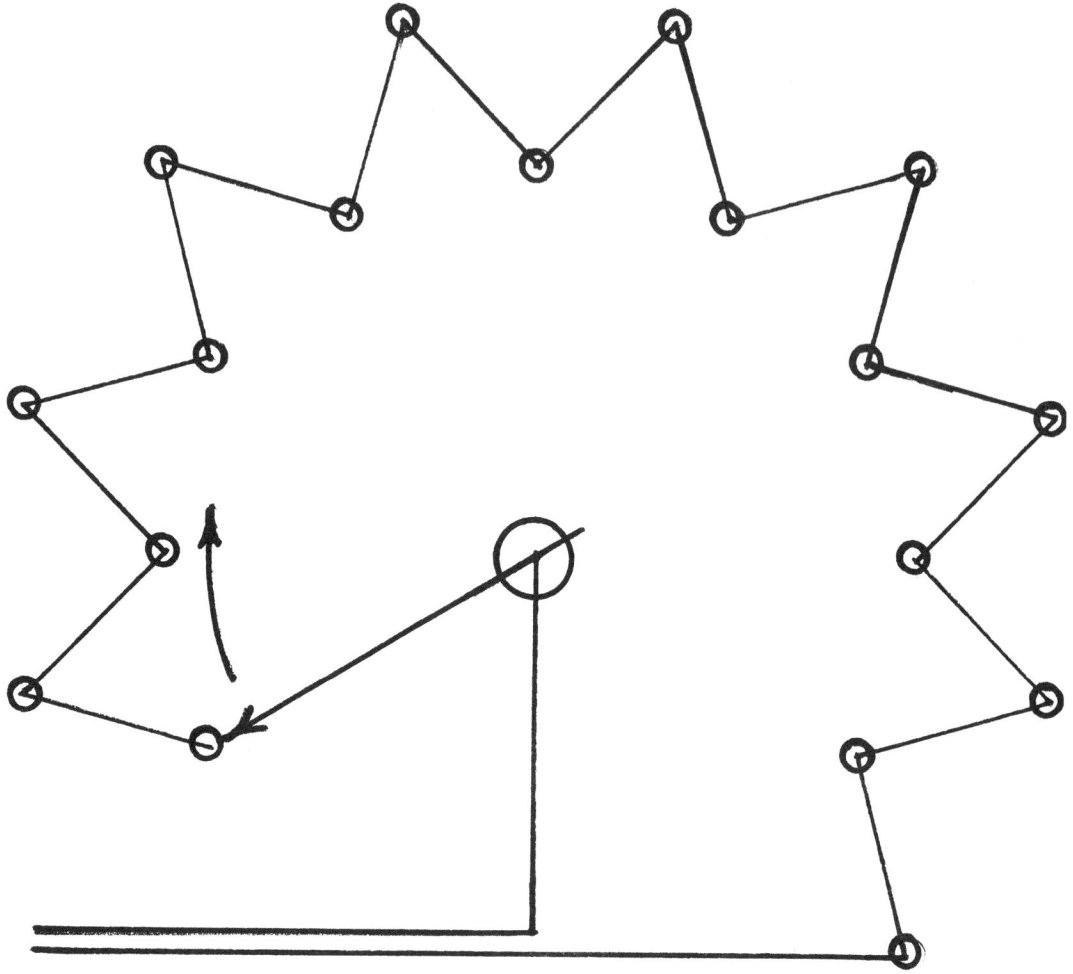

Figure 44

decrease the electrical current in a circuit by adding resistance. In fact, the more resistance you add, the lower the current becomes. It must seem logical to you, then, that you can take a highly resistant metal and introduce it into the circuit gradually to cut the current down to any amount you wish. That is the principle of the resistance dimmer.

In practice a resistance dimmer consists of a length of highly resistant wire, one end of which is connected to the electrical circuit. The other side of the circuit is connected to an arm or lever that slides up and down the length of the resistance wire, thereby increasing or decreasing the amount of resistance wire in the circuit. When the arm is at the end connected to the other side of the circuit, the maximum current will flow. As you move the arm away, you are reducing the current, because of the additional resistance you are introducing into the circuit, until it has been reduced to practically nothing. Most of the resistance dimmers you see today have the resistance wire installed in a circle, and the arm travels in an arc around the circle, as demonstrated in Figure 44. You can visualize how this works on the actual dimmer by seeing the inside of one as shown in Figure 45.

Just as lamps have wattage ratings, so do resistance dimmers. They vary from 200 watts to 3,600 watts. The most common sizes are 500, 1,000, 1,500, and 2,000 watts. When using them you must know their wattage (they are usually labeled) because it

Dimmers—Resistance and Auto-Transformer / 65

tells you what their capacity is. The total wattage of the lighting instruments controlled by each dimmer must not exceed the rated wattage, or capacity, of the dimmer. In other words, if you have a 2,000-watt dimmer, you may use it with two 1,000-watt instruments, or one 1,000-watt and two 500-watt instruments, or four 500-watt instruments, or any other combination adding up to 2,000 watts. It is a safety hazard to exceed the capacity of a dimmer.

If you have ever seen resistance dimmers, you have probably seen them lined up in rows, or banks, as shown in Figure 46. You

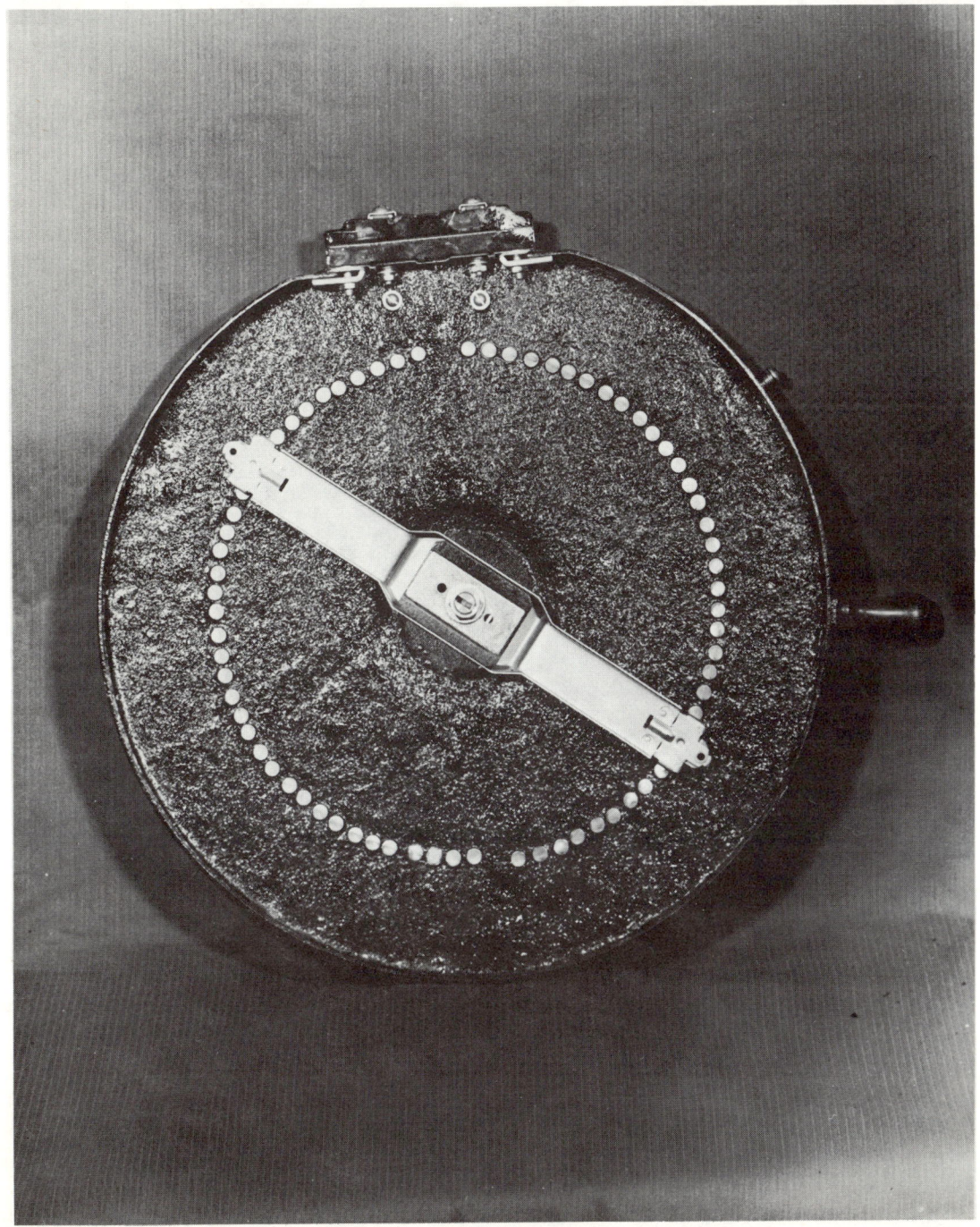

Figure 45

66 / **Practical Stage Lighting**

Figure 46

may have wondered how many people are required to operate all of the levers during a production that requires many light changes. The answer, by today's standards, is "too many"; but it is possible to use an interlocking system that allows one person to control eight or ten dimmers.

The system involves a handle on each dimmer arm that may be rotated a one-quarter turn to lock, or unlock, each arm to a shaft that runs to four or five dimmers. The shaft, in turn, is controlled by its own arm, or master handle, which is larger than the dimmer handles. By locking the handles to the shaft, you can operate several or all of them with the master handle. Yet by unlocking any of them you can operate it independently. You are able to set each dimmer independently at a different level and lock each one onto the shaft. You may then lower or raise them simultaneously by using the master handle. As you move the master handle to the position of each locked dimmer handle, it automatically locks onto the shaft and moves with the master. Any unlocked dimmer handle will remain in its set position, unaffected by the master.

Resistance dimmers are considered obsolete, even archaic, but you may still find them in use in many old theatres and school auditoriums. Their main disadvantages are: 1) Like any electrical resistant material, they generate considerable heat, causing discomfort to the operator and the possibility of fire; 2) in using the interlocking system, all locked dimmers must be dimmed to the same point without allowing for different rates of dimming of individual dimmers (a technique called proportionate dimming, which will be discussed later in this chapter); 3) although the maximum rating of a dimmer must not be exceeded, a resistance dimmer must be loaded to its maximum whether you need the lights or not. If you have less than the rated wattage in a circuit with a resistance dimmer, it cannot be dimmed below a certain point. The lower the wattage in the circuit, the brighter the lights will be when the dimmer is all the way down. In other words, if you use a 1,000-watt dimmer to control a 750-watt light, it is necessary to add another 250 watts to the circuit if you wish to operate it properly. This is usually done by connecting up an unused lighting instrument as a "dummy load." They are sometimes referred to as "phantoms" or "black boxes." The term black box is used because the light is frequently covered with a wooden or metal box painted black inside and out to keep the unwanted light from shining where it might ruin an effect.

To understand what an auto-transformer is, we must look at some more characteristics of electricity. This can be done simply and without getting technical. First of all, a conductor with electricity flowing through it is surrounded by a magnetic field. When the electricity stops flowing, the magnetic field disappears. This characteristic underlies the principle of the electromagnet, which is merely a piece of iron placed in the magnetic field of a conductor. The iron becomes a magnet when the electricity is on and demagnetizes when the electricity is off. Such a magnet operates the clapper on an electric doorbell or door chimes.

Another interesting electrical characteristic results if you place a loop of conducting wire in the magnetic field caused by an

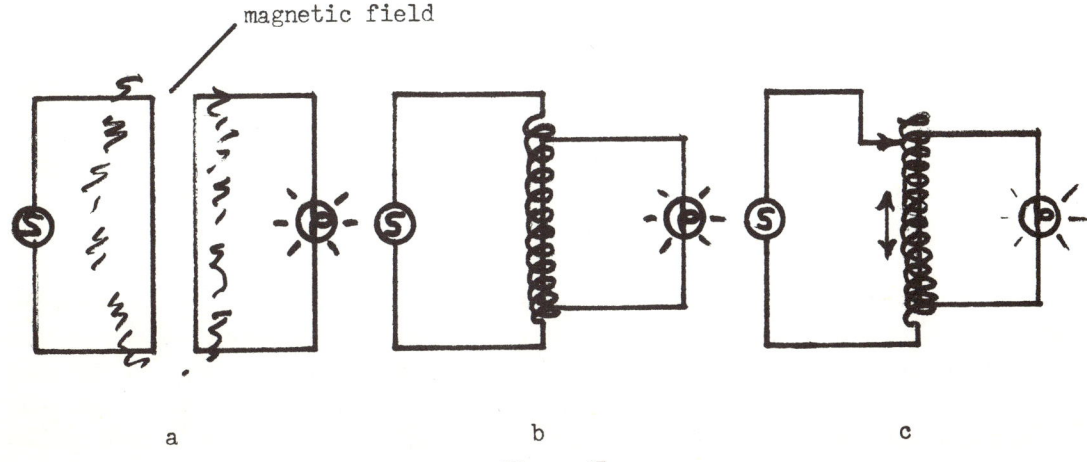

Figure 47

electrical circuit. In doing so, you will induce a current of electricity in the loop without any other source of power. This phenomenon is diagrammed in Figure 47-a. In order to create a magnetic field strong enough to have a significant effect, it is necessary to twist the wire into a spiral winding called a coil. The wire through which the current will be induced is then inserted inside the coil, as shown in Figure 47-b. The outside coil is called the primary coil and the inner wire is called the secondary. This device is called a transformer.

The voltage in the secondary will be determined by the number of turns of the wire in the primary coil. By increasing the turns, a higher voltage is induced. By decreasing the turns, the induced voltage is lowered. A transformer with a wire that may be moved from one end of the primary coil to the other end, is called the auto-transformer or, sometimes, a variable transformer. As you can see in Figure 47-c, the movement of the wire will increase or decrease the number of turns in the primary coil, causing changes in voltage in the secondary circuit.

It now follows that if we install an auto-transformer in our lighting circuit and plug our lights into the secondary circuit, we can use the device as a dimmer. Decreases in voltage in the secondary will cause the light to dim down, and increases will cause it to become brighter. Most auto-transformer dimmers that are used on the stage are referred to by one of the two most popular trade names: "Powerstats," manufactured by Superior Electric Company; or "Variacs," manufactured by General Radio Company. Figure 48 shows a typical auto-transformer.

The auto-transformer resolves the three disadvantages of the resistance dimmer. First, since they do not use resistance wire, they do not generate excessive heat. Secondly, you may control a group of them with a larger dimmer that will dim them down, or up, without moving the setting on any of the individual dimmers. This feature allows you to dim proportionately.

Proportionate dimming is the effect you get when all lights start to decrease in intensity at the same time and continue to decrease until they are out. For instance, suppose you have a setting of three instruments, each on its own dimmer. Instrument A is full up, instrument B is two-thirds up, and instrument C is one-half up. As you dim all three down on a master dimmer, they will remain in the same proportions. B will always be two-thirds as bright as A, and C will always be one-half as bright as A until they are out. The same proportionate situation would exist if you were to dim them back up again.

Finally, since the auto-transformer varies the voltage rather than the amperage, the dimmer will work just as effectively whether it carries its maximum rated wattage or a wattage less than its maximum. No phantom or dummy load is required. You can obtain auto-transformer dimmers in wattages from 500 to 5,000. The 5,000-watt dimmers may be obtained in groups that are "stacked" or "ganged." Any number up to six may be stacked together (at the factory) for a maximum capacity as high as 30,000 watts.

You may obtain auto-transformer dimmers as individual units that you can plug into any outlet. This style contains outlets in the secondary into which you can plug the cables to connect to your lighting instruments. Or, if you prefer, you can obtain them with screw terminals so that you can have them installed on, and wired into, your control board. Most manufacturers also sell complete control board units containing the number and size dimmers you wish.

This type of dimmer has two other advantages. It consumes considerably less current than the resistance dimmer, making it less expensive to operate. It is also smaller, occupying less space than the resistance dimmer. Its disadvantages are that it is a more expensive piece of equipment and is more delicate and more difficult to repair. If you are careful, however, it will last quite a long time without the need for repair.

Dimmers—Resistance and Auto-Transformer / 69

Figure 48

In addition to the normal precautions against overloading and physical damage, you must remember two other precautions: 1) Do not switch the current on unless the dimmer is turned all of the way off. A sudden surge of electricity may cause an arc between the primary and secondary that could burn out or "fuse" the coil. 2) Do not bang the control dial at the ends of its turn (turn it gently). The stops on each end cannot be built strong enough to resist such banging and they will break, or move out of position, making the dial inoperable.

Chapter IX

DIMMERS—ELECTRONIC

As stated at the beginning of Chapter VIII, there are two remaining categories of dimmers. We have broadly classified them as reactance dimmers and electron-tube dimmers. They are both considered electronic dimmers. Those of you who have some knowledge of electricity may immediately object because you know that reactance is an electrical rather than an electronic term. Even though reactance is electrical, we shall refer to certain electronic dimmers as reactance dimmers because they evolved from, and are based upon, the principles of reactance. As a matter of fact, in a way, even the electron-tube dimmers evolved from the reactance dimmer, as you will see as we trace the history of electronic dimmers.

The reactance dimmer was introduced prior to the use of the auto-transformer dimmer. It works on a principle similar to the auto-transformer dimmer except that the number of turns in the primary coil remains constant. Instead of varying the turns in the primary, it operates by moving the secondary into and out of the magnetic field of the primary. The voltage is increased when more of the secondary is moved into the field. The construction is simple. The operation is economical. The device, however, is extremely bulky and has been passed over in favor of the lighter, smaller auto-transformer.

The reactance dimmer manufacturers have attempted to remain in the field and have modified the reactance dimmer to a device known as the saturable-core reactor. In the saturable-core reactor, the secondary is stationary and another coil is introduced into the primary field. The additional coil is connected to a direct current, whereas the primary coil is powered by alternating current. It was found that the higher the voltage fed into the direct current coil, the lower the voltage induced in the primary.

The only task was to devise a suitable method of converting alternating current to a controllable direct current for the new coil. They decided to use electronic rectifier tubes because they not only converted the current but could also be used as a means of controlling the voltage of that current. This incidental use of electron tubes was the first introduction of electronics into theatrical dimming devices. The rectifier tubes and their circuitry require a very small amount of current and use small components. As a result it is possible to install a large number of dimmer circuits on a small control panel, making remote control practicable. In addition, this reactor consumes very little current, does not produce much heat, and will properly dim any load within its rated capacity.

The disadvantages are that its cost is prohibitive except to large, commercial theatres, and it is not as easy to maintain as the manufacturers claim. Although the control panel contains small, light equipment, considerable bulky equipment is involved in the system. Because of these disadvantages, you may never see a saturable-core reactor. A number of them, however, are still in operation in large theatres where they were installed in the 1920's.

Let us turn our attention, now, to the rectifier tubes that controlled the direct current to the direct current coil in the saturable-core reactor. Changing alternating current to direct current is only one of many functions performed by electron tubes. It is not necessary to know the principle of, or the science behind, the electron tube to understand that the rectifier tube, in itself, can serve as a dimmer. Without discussing the technicalities, let us just say that each tube has more than one electrical circuit flowing into it. In the rectifier tube, one of the circuits carries a relatively powerful alternating current and another circuit carries a low-voltage direct current. Small changes in the direct-current voltage will cause inverse changes in the alternating-current voltage just as happens in the saturable-core reactor. You can see how the tube itself might be used as a dimmer.

Prior to World War II, however, rectifier tubes were not powerful enough to supply electricity to theatrical lighting instruments. During the war, a rectifier tube was developed for military use so that it could handle high voltages. It is called a thyratron tube.

In 1947, George Izenour at Yale University devised a dimmer using a pair of thyratron tubes, thereby creating the first fully electronic dimmer. This, of course, was the first electron-tube type of dimmer. The system has all of the remote-control advantages of the saturable-core reactor and, although the tube banks are large and space-consuming, it is not as bulky. It is certainly considerably lighter in weight and not quite as costly to build. One of the disadvantages is the great amount of heat generated by the thyratron tubes. This is partly compensated for by the fact that they can be controlled remotely and are usually installed in an out-of-the-way fireproof area where the heat causes no inconvenience or danger. Another disadvantage is that, like any electron tube, they require a warmup period before they can be used. They also require frequent expert attention because they tend to drift out of adjustment. This factor, in addition to the need for periodic replacement, creates a costly maintenance situation.

The system was popular, however, and several university and community theatres, as well as a few high schools, installed the Izenour switchboard. Many are in use. Some have been installed in new theatres as late as the mid-1960's.

The reactance people, who had competed with the auto-transformer dimmer, refused to drop out of the picture. The main factor that kept them in contention was the development of the magnetic amplifier in the 1950's. Like the thyratron tube, this device was originally developed for other uses, mostly industrial. It actually is a refinement of the saturable-core reactor and needs no warmup time, nor does it give off much heat. Unlike the saturable-core reactor, it has unlimited, maintenance-free life. On the other hand, like the saturable-core reactor, it is bulky, heavy, and costly to build.

The latest development in theatrical dimmers is classified as an electron-tube dimmer. It does not use tubes, but does use a substitute device that functions as a thyratron tube. In this day when the terms "transistor" and "solid-state device" are common household words, it will probably mean something to you to know that the thyratron tube has been replaced by a transistor, and the resulting device is known as a solid-state dimmer or "Silicon Controlled Rectifier (SCR)."

In view of its popularity, the chances are strong that your theatre already has one. If not, it is quite probable that someday you will work on a stage that has the SCR dimmer. For that reason, perhaps it will help you to understand a little more about it.

First of all, scientists have discovered that certain materials will perform like electron tubes if they have been cut into very small wafer-shaped objects, properly treated and installed with the correct circuitry. One of these materials, silicon, can be made to perform as a rectifier tube and controlled as the thyratron tube is controlled. It is called a silicon controlled rectifier. It is actually a silicon rectifier under control and not, as some people think, a rectifier controlled by silicon. It is commonly referred to as the SCR dimmer. It has a much greater capacity than the normal transistor that is installed in your pocket radio. It has all the advantages of the magnetic amplifier, but it is extremely small and lightweight. It is less expensive than either the magnetic amplifier or the thyratron tube dimmer.

The SCR is very sensitive to overloading as well as to high temperatures. Protection against these situations presents no problem, however, thanks to the use of special fuses and built-in fans. Another problem that you may encounter with the SCR is the tendency it has to create a vibration in the lamp filaments, causing a distinct and bothersome humming sound. This is caused by the rapid switching action that occurs in the SCR dimmer. Most manufacturers, however, will provide a special filter that corrects the vibration.

SCR dimmers are available as packaged units, or control boards, containing anywhere from six to almost any number of dimmer circuits. They will be discussed in the next chapter. The prices start below $1,500 for a simple six-dimmer unit including all circuitry and control units.

At the time of this writing, the SCR is the latest and most suitable device for use as a dimmer. It seems to be the ultimate in design and technique. In view of the rate of scientific advancement, however, there is no telling what the future may bring in advanced methods of controlling the intensity of stage lighting instruments. It is not inconceivable, for instance, that someday each light instrument will have a self-contained dimmer that might be radio-controlled by a small, pocket-sized controller that could be carried around anywhere in the theatre building. Certainly other advanced ideas may be developed in the future. You may have some yourself!

Chapter X

SWITCHBOARDS AND CONSOLES

In the last two chapters we discussed dimmer units, but also mentioned dimmer banks and solid-state control units. We discussed them, however, only to the extent necessary to describe the operation and virtues of the various types of dimmer. Although the dimmers are a most important component on the control board, there are other important devices. This chapter is devoted to the correlation of all the devices on the control board and the various aspects of the operation of the complete system.

Various names are used for control boards. The most common are "switchboards," "dimmer banks," "control panels," "switch panels," and "consoles." We shall, for the sake of clarity, call them all "control boards" and divide them into two types. One type we will refer to as "switchboards" and the other type we will refer to as "consoles." The switchboards contain dimmers that are controlled directly. The consoles contain remote control (electronic) devices.

A switchboard consists of three parts, namely, the dimmer bank, the switch panel, and the interconnecting panel. The dimmer bank consists of the rows of dimmers, either resistance, reactance, or auto-transformer. They are usually installed in rows of three to six dimmers with the master dimmer for each row on the end, or in the center, of the row. You should identify each row by a letter and each dimmer by a number in the same way you identify the seats in the theatre. It is recommended also that on, or near, each dimmer handle you affix a label indicating the rated capacity in watts of that individual dimmer. Systems of color coding sometimes aid in quick identification of the proper control. The panel adjacent to each dimmer handle, or wheel, is calibrated with markings from 0 to 10 or 0 to 100. This feature is to allow you to record the precise setting of each dimmer for each scene.

When operating dimmers, remember that the audience will not notice small changes in intensity if they are made slowly. If you have to make a significant change quickly, don't worry about hitting the precise setting on each dimmer. After you have made the change, you can slowly adjust each dimmer individually to the exact setting without the audience's being aware that the lights are changing.

Switch panels are frequently designed so that the switches are adjacent to the individual dimmer that they control. You may, however, occasionally find a switchboard with the switch panel set aside from the dimmer handles. In any case, the panel will contain, at the least, an "on-off" switch and a fusing device for each dimmer circuit. If there are several banks, or groups, of dimmers there will probably be a switch to control each group. In addition there should always be a master switch to control the entire

73

dimmer bank. The master switch is referred to as the "blackout" switch, since it is used when a blackout is called for.

If the dimmers are auto-transformer or direct-controlled reactance dimmers, "on-off" switches are not usually used in the individual dimmer circuits. Instead, a three-position switch is used. In addition to the "on" and "off" positions, the third position is usually called "master" or "bank" and it connects each dimmer circuit to the master dimmer for proportional dimming. To operate the dimmers, you place the switch in the "on" position when you wish to work the dimmer individually and in the "bank" position when you wish it to work with the group of dimmers under control of the master dimmer. Some switch panels use two separate switches instead. One is a regular "on-off" switch for the individual dimmer and the other will be a "bank" "on-off" switch to put the dimmer into, or take it out of, the group circuit.

Every circuit will have a fuse. Fuses are safety devices that react when a circuit is overloaded, grounded out, overheated, or "short-circuited" (making contact with another circuit). They indicate these conditions by opening the circuit, thereby cutting off the electrical current. This situation is commonly referred to as a "blown fuse." Before replacing, or resetting, the fuse, you must determine the cause of the failure and remedy the situation.

The three common types of fuse are shown in Figure 49. They are the plug fuse, the cartridge fuse, and the circuit breaker. The plug fuse is a common household fuse that you may easily screw into and out of the circuit, since it fits into a screw socket. When you use a fuse, you are inserting into the circuit a strip of resistance metal that has a low melting point. When an unsafe condition creates enough heat in the circuit to become dangerous, the metal in the fuse is the first part of the circuit to melt, opening the circuit and cutting off the current before the heat becomes extreme enough to cause a fire.

The cartridge fuse is similar to the plug fuse in the way it functions. As you can see, the shape differs, and it is inserted by fitting the metal ends into tight-fitting brackets that clamp over each end. They hold the fuse very tightly so that it is sometimes necessary, and always safer, to use a tool to remove and insert the fuse. Most electricians have fuse pincers that look like pliers but are made of an insulating material. You may use insulated pliers, but *do not* try to pry the fuse out with a screwdriver or other metal device.

The circuit breaker, although it serves the same purpose, is not really a fuse. It is more properly called a relay. A relay is a device that moves automatically to open or close an electrical circuit. The circuit breaker type of fuse opens when the circuit becomes overheated beyond its capacity, and you can reset it by hand after the difficulty has been corrected. It is built into the control switch and causes the control switch to snap into the "off" position. In order to reset the relay, you must move the switch to a third position, "reset." It may then be moved to the "on" position and it remains there. If you do not reset, the switch will spring to the "off" position each time you try to turn it on.

All fuses are rated in amperes to show the amount of current they will carry before they open the circuit. Fuses used on the stage range from 10 amps to 100 amps. Most circuits are protected with 15- or 20-amp fuses. Usually fuses of 60 amps or more are cartridge type. When you wish to determine the maximum wattage to put in a circuit, you simply multiply the amperage of the fuse by the voltage. For instance, if a 110-volt circuit has a 15-amp fuse, you may plug in your lights not to exceed 1,650 watts. Make sure, however, that your dimmer is rated to carry 1,650 watts. It is a good idea to label each switch showing 1) the dimmer it controls, 2) the capacity of the dimmer in wattage, and 3) the amperage for which it is fused. A numbering system identical to the numbering system for the dimmers is recommended to help you identify each switch.

Switchboards and Consoles / 75

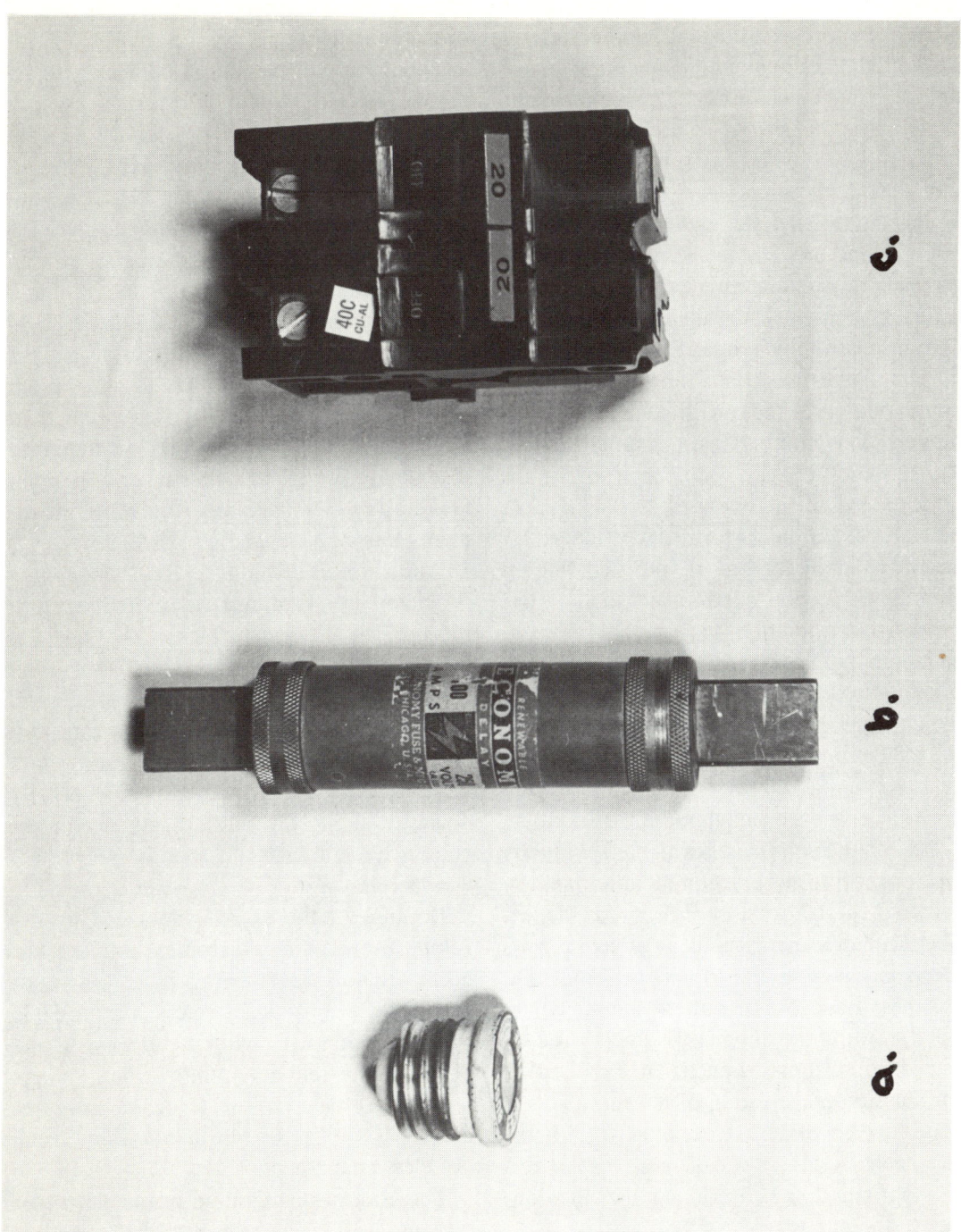

Figure 49

The third and final part of a switchboard is the interconnecting panel. In many cases, especially in school auditoriums, the switchboards are wired permanently to the lighting instruments, and no interconnecting panels are used. Such a condition is undesirable and should be corrected, because it allows you little, if any, flexibility in the use of your dimmer circuits.

An interconnecting panel is a panel of outlets that are connected directly to the dimmers. It contains two to four receptacles for each dimmer. Plug the cables leading to lighting instruments and other electrical devices into the interconnecting panel so that you may control them with your dimmers as desired. The interconnecting panel may be situated on the rear, side, or front of the switchboard. In many cases it is a separate unit situated adjacent to the switchboard, or anywhere in the theatre. If your switchboard is in the projection booth, it is usually a less expensive installation to put the interconnecting panel backstage. On the other hand, it is more convenient to have it close to the switchboard, making it possible for you to change circuits as you wish during the course of a production without having to move too far away from the switchboard.

Interconnecting panels are made with any type of receptacle to accommodate pin connectors, Twist-Locks, or Edison connectors. The receptacles are usually arranged in rows corresponding to the dimmer banks and switches. Each set of outlets should be labeled showing the dimmer to which it is connected, the wattage capacity of the dimmer, and the amperage rating of the fuse. This is important so that, as you plug your lights into each circuit, you can easily make certain that you do not overload either the dimmer or the circuit.

In addition to the above features, a switchboard should have extra outlets with individual switches and fuses, for lights and devices that you do not wish to dim but do wish to control with an "on-off" switch on your switch panel. Some switchboards have individual pilot lights for each switch. You may not wish to incur the expense of installing this luxury, since a good switchboard operator will know the positions of his switches without needing a pilot light to remind him. The switchboard must be illuminated so that the operator can see all controls and, even more important, if it is backstage, the light must not in any way interfere with your stage lighting effects.

The major disadvantage of the switchboard is that you cannot obtain the maximum use from each dimmer. When a light is being used, you cannot take it out of its dimmer circuit without first turning it off. The dimmer, therefore, is tied up with a light that does not require an intensity change over a period of time when you might make a use of that dimmer on other instruments that require changes in intensity.

Another disadvantage arises from the problems in installing the switchboard in the projection booth, which is the ideal location so the operator can see his lighting from the same viewpoint as the audience. The heavy-duty equipment and wiring that is necessary for each dimmer results in a costly installation. The switches are usually noisy enough to distract the audience unless you have the luxury of a soundproof projection booth.

Because of those disadvantages, the development of the electronic dimmers has been a major breakthrough in lighting control. With electronic dimmers it is possible to change dimmers without turning off the lights and to remotely control the dimmers with low-voltage power at your console, requiring less expensive installation and using noiseless components.

The control boards used in the electronic systems are called "consoles" because they can be built, and usually are, in small, compact, desk-shaped cabinets. The operator may sit at the console and operate it while looking over the top of it at the stage through a projection-booth window as shown in Figure 50.

Switchboards and Consoles / 77

The consoles consist of two units and, although manufacturers use varying terminology, the most common terms are "the dimmer unit" and "the control unit." Figure 51 shows a typical dimmer unit. There is one for each dimmer, and they are usually ganged together to form a cabinet or module. In addition to the dimmers, it contains fuses and anywhere from two to four outlets for each dimmer. All high-voltage circuits

Figure 50

78 / Practical Stage Lighting

are contained in the dimmer unit, which you may install anywhere in the theatre. The dimmer unit connects directly to your source of power. In addition to the receptacles for your lighting instruments, it also has a cable that connects it to the control unit. This cable carries the low-voltage circuits, and you can obtain the length you need at a moderate cost.

You may place the dimmer unit in the console, but one of the advantages of the system is that you can have it installed in a suitable backstage location, whereas the console can be placed in your projection booth or anywhere else that is suitable to your requirements. The cost of doing this involves only the moderate price of the additional cable. Since only low voltage is involved, high-power components are not required in the control unit. Silent operating switches are used.

All sorts of designs and features are available from a number of manufacturers, including portable control units that may be moved anywhere at any time as long as you have provided a long enough cable. The simplest, least expensive models operate in a manner similar to the old type of switchboards. There is a control lever and an "on-off" switch for each dimmer. There may be a large number of dimmers. They are packaged in multiples of three or six. It is not very practical to try to use a system with less than six dimmers. You operate them in the same way you would operate any switchboard.

The SCR dimmer has made certain features possible that cannot be found in other

Figure 51

Switchboards and Consoles / 79

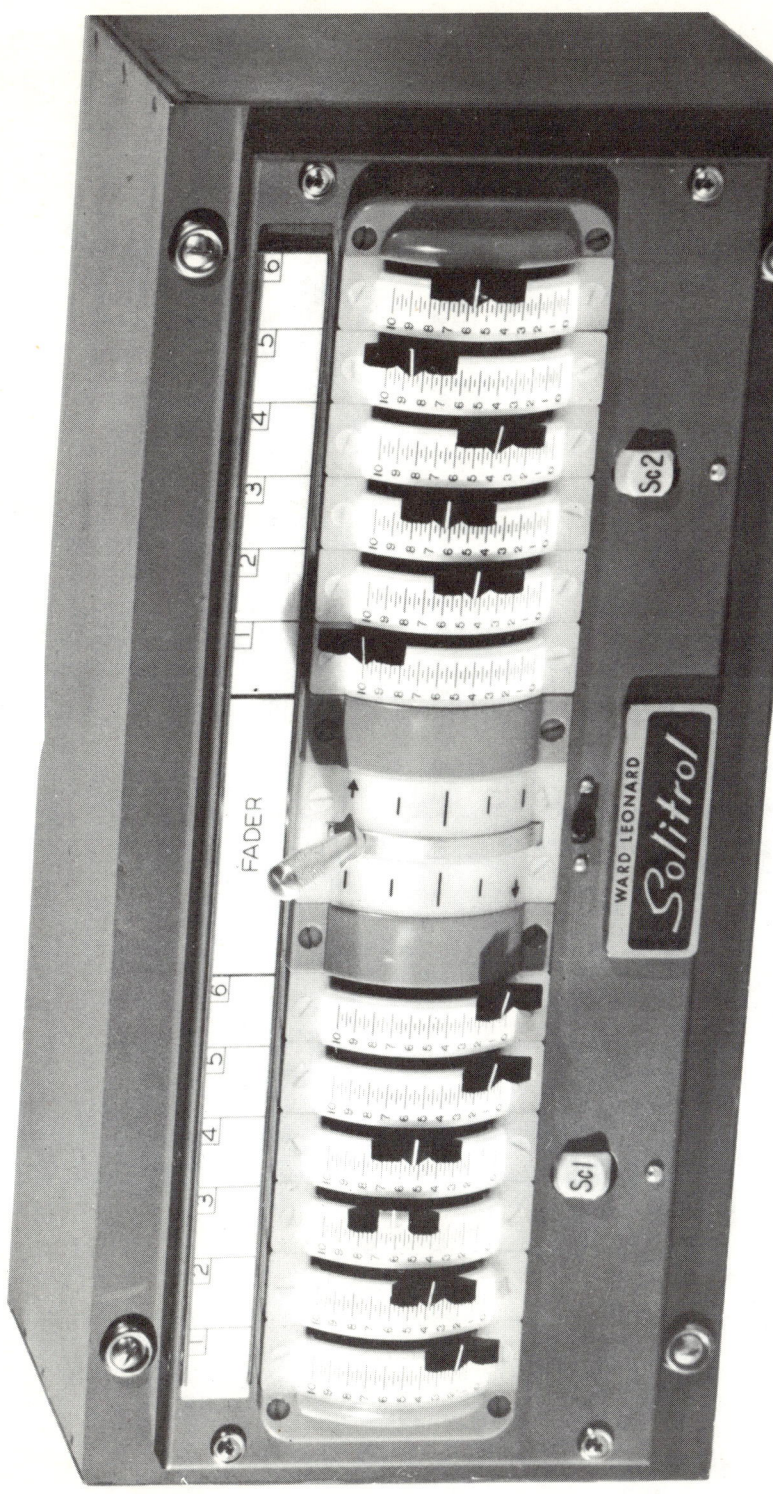

Figure 52

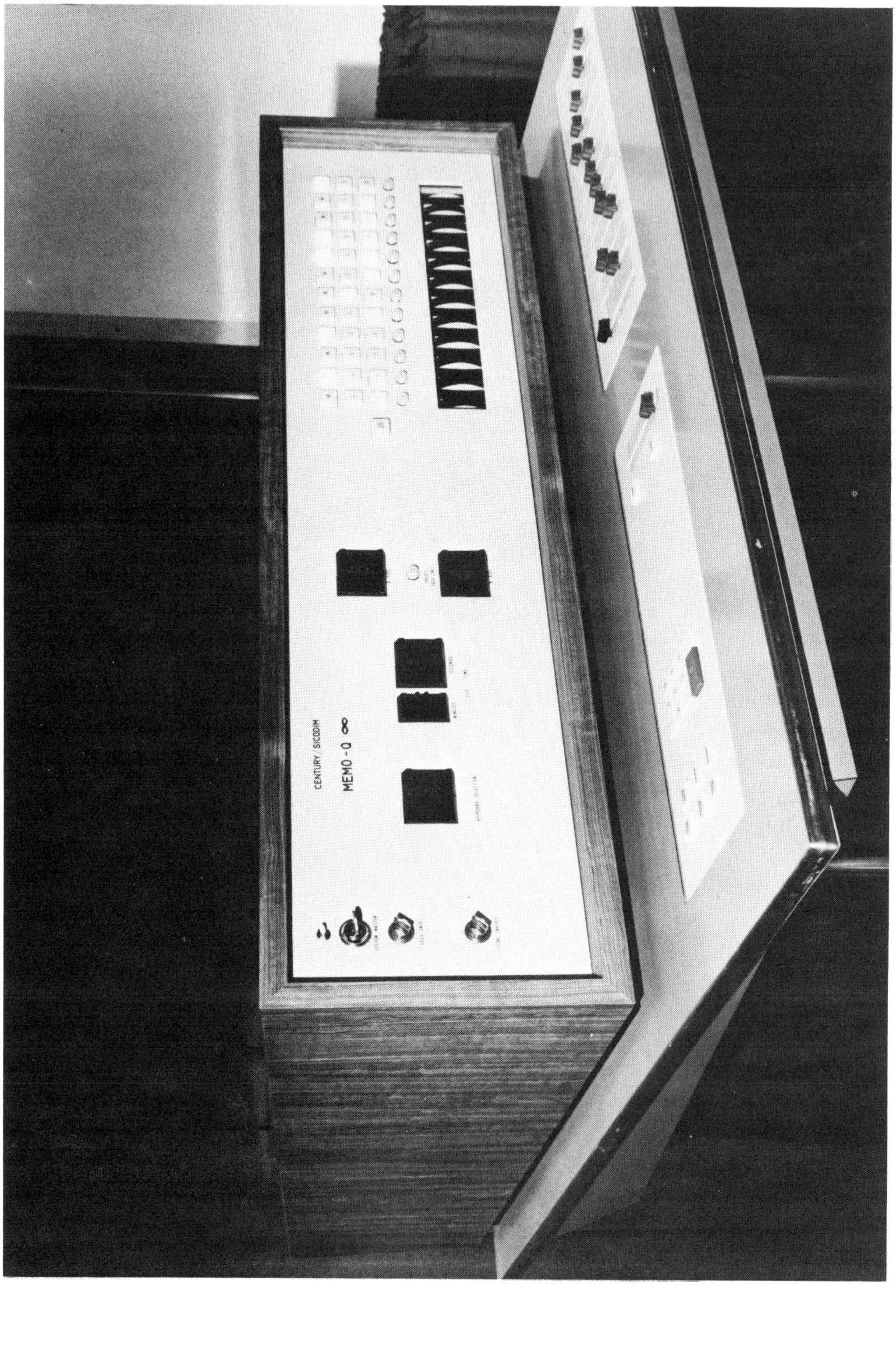

80 / **Practical Stage Lighting**

Figure 53

dimmer systems. The cross-fader is the most popular of these. On the face of the control unit are (see Figure 52) two sets of control levers, only one of which will control a bank of dimmers at a given time. On the other set of levers you can preset the light setting for the next scene. The cross-fader is the lever you use to change the dimmers from one set of control levers to the other. You may do this manually at whatever speed you wish to effect a slow, gradual change in intensities, or an instant change. More sophisticated systems have rows upon rows of control levers, making it possible to preset any number of scenes and lighting changes for an entire production, which may involve many complicated changes in lighting. All you need do is cross-fade from one scene to the next, using the cross-fader provided for each row of levers when the cues come up for each change in lights.

If you can afford it, you may have a console with motorized cross-faders and speed controls so that you need only press a button on cue and the cross-faders will automatically operate at whatever speed you have preset for each lighting change. With equipment of this type, you can change lighting intensities for any number of instruments throughout a complete production merely by pushing a single button each time you wish the lights to start changing. Needless to say, we are now talking about expensive equipment.

The most sophisticated system on the market at the time of this writing is called the Memo-Q,* manufactured by Century-Strand, Incorporated. It is a computerized console with motorized controls. It can be used for virtually an unlimited number of dimmers and presets. It has a single master push button, which instantly records either a single circuit or all of the values of a complete lighting setup. You can recall presets at will in any selected sequence at any desired speed. This is invaluable for rehearsals, when taking pictures and setting lighting instruments. You may record numbered cues at random and have them played back instantly in their proper numerical sequence. Or you can change their sequence to skip directly into any selected scene at will. While one scene is playing, you can monitor other presets and, if you wish, make changes in them for upcoming scenes. At any time during rehearsal or performance you may override the automatic settings and operate the controls manually on one, several, or all of the presets. Figure 53 shows the demonstration model of the control unit for this remarkable system.

---

* Patent pending, Century-Strand, Inc.

Chapter XI

BUDGET CONTROLS

Regardless of what type of theatrical organization you are associated with, you will find that certain persons and rules limit or prohibit the use of makeshift equipment. This was mentioned in Chapter VII when we were discussing homemade instruments. Control boards, because they are of a more permanent nature than the portable lighting instruments, are subject to even stricter rules and closer investigation.

Because of this, do not spend any money on materials and equipment unless you know that the proper authorities will approve of the construction. Those authorities may be local building inspectors, insurance underwriters, or your own maintenance engineers and administration. In any case, the administration of your organization will know whose approval is required and you should consult them and point out to them that the proper authorities must be satisfied.

Some of the devices described in this chapter are not approved by local authorities. If you build them as described and operate them properly, they are perfectly safe. The objections to them are that they do not have enough built-in safeguards to protect against improper, or careless, operation. In some cases you will find that a thorough discussion of your plans and problems with the duly constituted authorities will result in some suggestions from them that will be within your capabilities and still meet their requirements. Frequently the use of heavier cable or additional fuses will satisfy them. It may cost a little more, but still not as much as it would cost to buy manufactured equipment.

Not many dimmers may be homemade unless you are a qualified electrician. The best known is called the "water barrel," or "salt-water," dimmer. It is the oldest type of dimmer that we know of. As recently as the early 1930's, it was still in use in some American nonprofessional theatres, and to some extent in theatres in England and France. It works on the principle that salt water acts as an electrical resistor.

To make a salt-water dimmer you must build or obtain a watertight tank of nonmetallic material. Plastic, glass, or ceramic are ideal. You may use wood, but you must caulk all joints, cracks, and holes with pitch, and it is a good idea to paint the interior with marine or deck paint. A suitable size would result in inside dimensions of 3" wide, 18" long, and 6" deep, as shown in Figure 54.

Attach a copper plate to the far end of the tank on the inside. Make the copper plate 3" square and install it on the lower half of the end of the tank, so that when you fill the tank with 4" of water, the plate will be completely submerged. Connect the plate to one leg of your circuit. Put a control switch and a fuse between the source of power and the plate.

Next, make a paddle out of insulation ma-

Budget Controls / 83

terial. Wood is satisfactory. Make the rectangular portion of the paddle 3″ wide and 6″ high with a 4″ handle above that. Attach another copper plate to the face of the paddle. Make this plate the same size as the first one and attach it to the lower half of the paddle so that you can place it directly against the stationary plate. Connect the plate on the paddle to an 18″ length of insulated wire. Attach the other end of the wire to an outlet on the near end of the tank, into which you may plug your lighting instrument cable. Connect the other terminal of the outlet to the other leg of your circuit, thereby completing the circuit.

Your paddle must have a crosspiece, as shown in Figure 54; this is placed just under the 6″ height, so that it will rest on top of the sides of the tank. Fill your tank with brine water to the 4″ mark. Hold the paddle as tightly against the stationary plate as you can and mark the position of the paddle's crosspiece on the sides of the tank. Cut notches opposite each other on the top of each side of the tank so that the paddle fits tightly up against the plate when the crosspiece is resting in the notches. In this position, the dimmer is "full-on." You may prefer to make slots or grooves in the sides of the tank to slide the paddle into. Notches are recommended instead, however, because you can use them without taking the paddle out of the brine, thereby opening the circuit.

Before we go any further, perhaps we should discuss the salt-water solution. It will vary depending upon the amount of current, the "hardness" of the water, and other factors. It is a good idea to start with a tablespoon of salt (household variety is satisfactory) to each quart of water. The next step is to move the paddle toward the near end of the tank until the light you wish to control is completely out. If it fails to go out, add more salt. When you find the "out" position, notch the sides of the tank again and you can set your paddle (control handle) in the "out" position. After that, it is a simple matter to use the same method and notch the sides of the tank to set each intensity level that you wish to use between "full-on" and "out."

As you have probably concluded, you will have to build a separate salt-water dimmer for each circuit you wish to control. They are recommended at best as temporary devices until you are able to obtain better dimmers. Their disadvantages are many. Since safety is of major importance, let us discuss, first, the disadvantage of the open tank. Many authorities will disapprove immediately of this aspect, which makes it possible for people inadvertently to dip their fingers into an open electrical circuit. Just as disastrous is the fact that objects can fall into the tank and cause dangerous short circuits. This disadvantage can be overcome by putting a cover on the tank. In that case you must provide a slot in the cover for the handle, or devise an inverted L-shaped paddle with the handle emerging from a slot near the top of one side of the tank. The L-shaped device causes operating difficulty when you need to reach the handle quickly. If you use a cover, always provide ventilation holes or slots for the fumes to escape.

Other disadvantages of the salt-water dimmers are their bulkiness and the fact that they emit unpleasant, although nontoxic, fumes. Since salt water has a strong corrosive effect upon metal, you must exercise constant care and frequently replace parts. Another bothersome characteristic is the fact that water evaporates, causing the salt to deposit on the sides of the tank, changing the consistency of the solution. You must check it periodically, change the brine frequently, and clean the components constantly.

Perhaps the most satisfactory way to economize on dimmers is by obtaining secondhand equipment. Everything we said in Chapter VII concerning used, and bargain, lighting instruments also applies to control equipment. You should know, however, that various government agencies make a heavy use of auto-transformer dimmers and it is possible to find suitable equipment in gov-

84 / Practical Stage Lighting

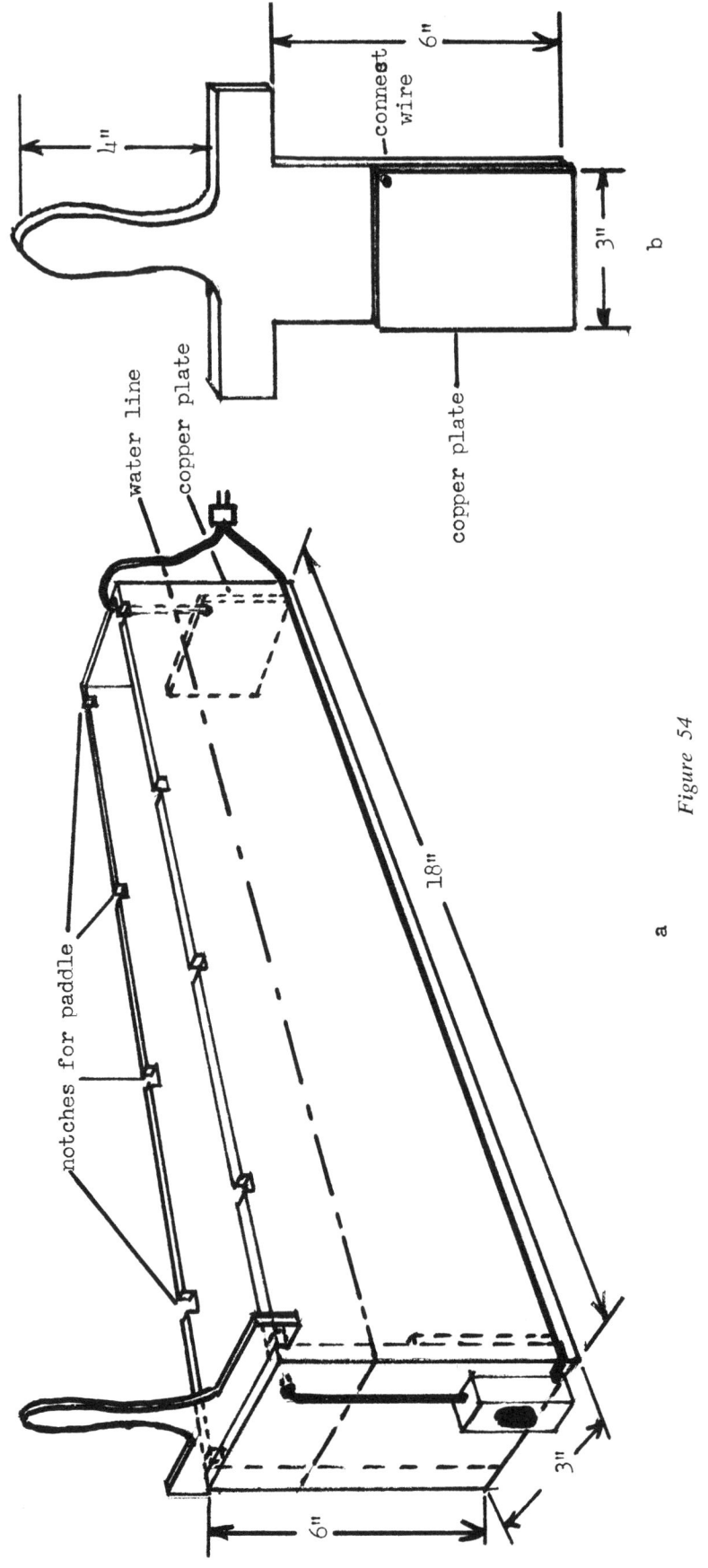

Figure 54

ernment surplus sales. If there is a surplus store in your area inquire about such items. If there is a government installation nearby, contact their surplus sales officer or purchasing agent. Frequently the agencies will have lists of surplus equipment available throughout the country. Lacking the above, you may be able to get information from purchasing agents of large corporations that are doing business with the government, or by writing directly to the General Services Administration, Washington, D.C.

When buying used auto-transformers, inspect the inside of the casings. Check the coil windings to see if any of the wires have fused together or are pitted from arcing. Before you buy, insist on operating each dimmer to see if it works properly. Check the stops at the end of the rotation of each control wheel or knob. If they turn very far beyond the end of the calibrations, it means that the stops are damaged or, at least, need adjustment or repair.

Whether you build it yourself, or can afford to obtain a factory-built system, you will want to have something to say about the design of your switchboard. Unless you are a qualified electrician, you cannot expect to design your control board by yourself. You can, however, protect yourself from the improper designs that are too frequently sold by people who have no theatrical comprehension. In the previous chapter we discussed the inflexibility of a control board that has no interconnecting panel or similar features. Too many auditoriums and school theatres have rows of dimmers permanently connected to borderlights and footlights, but no provision for dimmers to control houselights and other stage lights. The unfortunate aspect of this situation is that it doesn't cost any more to incorporate interconnecting features if they are included in the original installation.

Whether you construct the control board yourself, have it custom built, or buy it completely assembled from the factory, twelve considerations should be kept in mind, as follows:

1) You must follow rules of safety. All circuits must be insulated so that the operator cannot, even accidentally, touch an open circuit. Live receptacles, such as are found on many interconnecting panels, should be enclosed and provided with a lock. In fact, you should be able to lock the master switch so that only authorized people can energize the controls. All parts of all circuits must be adequately fused.

2) Many homemade boards are constructed of wood. If proper heat insulation is used, wooden supports and panels are quite safe; but, if at all possible, metal panels are preferable.

3) There should be some type of interconnecting panel or device that will allow you to use each dimmer with any of the lighting instruments on the stage at any time that you wish.

4) The individual dimmers and the entire control board must have high enough rated capacity to handle the maximum loads you will be using. You should be able to compute this yourself by dividing the wattage you will be using by the voltage of the system.

5) There should be a sufficient number of dimmers. Some experts feel that it is ideal to have a dimmer for each lighting instrument. That would be an unnecessary expenditure, since it is highly unlikely that you would ever need to change the intensity of all your instruments at once. In addition, you will usually control at least two, in some cases three, instruments with each dimmer for reasons that we shall discuss later. You should, however, try to obtain enough dimmers to handle at least half, but no more than 70 percent, of your instruments at one time.

6) Installing the dimmers in banks or groups is worth the expense. Each group should have its own master dimmer and switch.

7) Switches, dimmer handles, and fuses must be logically situated for the most convenient operation and they must be plainly labeled as discussed in the previous chapter.

8) The worklight for the switchboard

must operate when the master switch is off. Light fixtures or lamps that require a warmup or delayed starting time are less desirable.

9) A qualified electrician must ascertain whether the service is two-wire or three-wire and whether it is heavy enough to carry the total load to be handled by the control board. In some cases it will be necessary to run new, or additional, service from the main line for your new control board.

10) Consider location before you start work. Ideally the control board should be where the operator can see all of his effects as the audience sees them. If it must be backstage, try to elevate it so that the operator can see the stage over the heads of other people and, if possible, over the top of the highest scenery that is liable to be placed between the operator and the stage. In any case try to place the controls so that the operator can have them in front of him when he looks at the stage and/or at the person who is to relay his cues to him.

11) Consider the advantages of a portable switchboard. Portability involves weight, interconnectability, and, possibly, wheels. If traveling performances are a possibility, lightness in weight becomes important. If you are cramped for space, wheels on the control board will give you more flexibility. For a portable control board, the ability to connect it with various types of service is essential. Sometimes it is necessary to carry several types of connectors with you. Some electricians have alligator clips with insulated handles so that they can connect onto any terminal or bus bar. Always make sure the service you connect to is heavy enough to carry the load of your control board. If you use the board at various spots in your own theatre, it may be more practical to install an input cable long enough to reach to the farthest location, so that the board can be moved without disconnecting it from its source of power. Heavy-duty cable of this nature, however, is usually expensive.

12) Install an expandable control board. Even if you can afford everything you need now, allow space and service for future requirements. Although dimmer prices keep spiraling upward, you may find it necessary to add a few each year until you get what you need. Also consider the possibility of better, or more sophisticated, controls and try to plan so that they can be incorporated, if obtained, without losing too much of the present installation.

If you install a control board and get prices on equipment and materials, you will come to the conclusion that even at the cheapest, there are no such things as budget controls. To that extent, the title of this chapter is misleading. Unlike lighting instruments, it is impossible to obtain adequate control equipment without spending a lot of money. You can, however, save money by obtaining the most suitable equipment for your system. Moreover, you can avoid wasting the money you spend if you install it with the above twelve considerations in mind.

Chapter XII

THE USE OF COLOR

Up to this point we have dealt with all the qualities of theatrical lighting except color. Do not jump to the conclusion that this means that color is therefore the least important. As stated in Chapter I, color is of much significance for enhancing plausibility, setting mood, showing emphasis, and establishing picturization. It also allows us to avoid the harsh starkness created by white, uncolored light on the stage. Before discussing the means of using color, however, it is necessary to look at some of the characteristics of colored light.

First of all, color is found in two elements: pigment and light. When you were in elementary-school art classes you were told about colored pigment. You probably remember the three primary colors. Red, blue, and yellow. You know that by mixing them in the correct proportions you can obtain any other color in the spectrum. Do you remember that presence of all colors results in black and absence of color results in white? You may have forgotten, however, that complementary colors are any two colors that produce a shade of black (gray) when you mix them in equal proportions.

These fundamentals of pigment color are also important when we think in terms of colored light, but there are some unexpected differences. To begin with, the three primary light colors are red, blue, and *green*. By mixing them in the correct proportions, you can obtain any color in the spectrum. In addition, in direct opposition to pigment colors, the presence of all light colors results in white and the absence of light results in black. Just as in pigment, we have complementary light colors, but they are any two colors that produce *white* light when you mix them in equal proportions.

Before we go on, let us discuss another characteristic of colored light. We must consider the effect of colored light upon colored pigment. Colored light changes the apparent color of painted surfaces and fabrics. Sometimes it changes them in unexpected ways. But before we look at any guidelines, we must be aware of the problems we encounter when we try to identify colors. For instance, the appearance of a color frequently depends upon the texture or irregularity of the surface. An identical shade of red may appear to be three separate shades if one is on a wooden surface, one on a fabric, and one on a hard metallic surface. This is further complicated by the fact that colored light appears to vary in shade depending on both the texture of the surface it hits and the angle at which it hits that surface. Finally, if this is not confusing enough, various people identify colors differently. Apart from color blindness, some people see dark red as brown; you may see blue-green as blue, whereas I may see it as green. Light orange and dark yellow are also frequently confused.

Because of all the above factors, the only

way to determine how a yellow costume will really look under a blue light is to try it and see for yourself. Many experts, however, make their own charts showing the effect of light colors on pigment. You will have trouble finding any two such charts that agree on all combinations. The following chart, therefore, contains only basic colors upon which there seems to be the most agreement. It is intended for general guidance only and will not apply to all conditions.

light, however, is neither flattering nor natural-looking since it tends to eliminate all natural shadows. On the other hand, if we were to light the actor from one side only, half of his face and body would be in the dark, and visibility would be poor.

You are probably wondering what all of this has to do with color. It is simply that we use color to solve the problem. Most sets of complementary colors contain one warm, or bright, color and one cold, or dark, color.

LIGHT COLORS

		BLUE	GREEN	RED	AMBER
P I G M E N T S	BLUE:	Blue	Purplish-black	Black	Bluish-black
	YELLOW:	Black	Yellowish-green	Light red	Light orange
	RED:	Purple	Purplish-black	Red	Brownish-red
	GREEN:	Greenish-brown	Green	Black	Greenish-blue

One effect that everyone will agree upon is that white pigment reflects the color of the light that is hitting it. The conclusions that you can reach based upon the above are that you can obtain some startling and unexpected effects by combining colored lighting with colored pigments and that you can "paint" any color on a white surface by using colored lights.

Our next consideration, then, is how we can use these facts to achieve good lighting effects. You know that we have varied purposes for our lighting. We light the actors with our acting area lights; we set mood with our tonal lights; we light backgrounds with our cyclorama and backing lights; and we create certain illusions with our special-effects lights. Let us consider these one at a time.

In the acting areas we are chiefly concerned with visibility. We therefore use bright light that illuminates all sides of the actor that are seen by the audience. Such

If you use the warm complementary color from the side of the stage whence the light is supposed to emanate, and the cool complementary color from the shadowed side of the stage, the actor will be lighted on both sides; yet, by comparison, the cool color will give the illusion of shadow, the warm color will give the illusion of bright light and, since they complement each other, the front of the actor, where both colors blend, will be illuminated with natural-looking white light. This technique is called "cross-area" lighting and will be discussed further in Chapter XIV.

The mechanics of obtaining color in light will be discussed shortly, but first let us consider the use of color in tonal lighting. As stated earlier, color has symbolic meanings. Cool, dark colors create a somber, sad atmosphere, whereas light, bright colors make people feel happy and gay. Warm colors set a mood of comfort and security, whereas cold colors represent unpleasantness and fear. In order to establish those moods with your tonal lighting, you bathe the stage in such colors as red, green, blue, magenta, amber, or pink.

If you need to change mood frequently in a production, you should use three-circuit striplights as tonal lights. With one of the primary colors in each of the circuits, you can quickly and easily change the color of your tonal lights by varying the intensities of the colors with your dimmers. On the other hand, this arrangement ties up three dimmers, so if you do not have many color changes in your tonal lighting, it is better to use scoops and use the exact color for the mood you wish to set. If you have enough scoops, you can use two or three sets of colors when you need one, or two, mood changes. If you do not have striplights, you can use three sets of scoops, each set having one of the primary colors and each set controlled by its individual dimmer.

Backdrops and cycloramas are lighted by striplights, scoops, or a combination of both. If they are white, you should use the three primary colors in your lights. In that way you will be able to change the color of the backing as you wish merely by operating the dimmers. If the backing or cyclorama is colored, you will be limited in the variety of color combinations you can reflect from it. Do not be afraid to experiment and see what effects you can get on your backdrops using colored lights. If you have one that has been spattered with various colors (especially the pigment primaries) it is possible to obtain some interesting effects as you "paint" it with light.

Since a later chapter is devoted to special-effects lighting, little will be said about it here except to point out that certain colors, to be identified shortly, are used to simulate sunlight, moonlight, firelight, and other special effects.

Now that we know what we want to do with color, let us concentrate on how we get color in our stage lights. There are four ways, or media, of obtaining colored light. They are 1) paint or "lamp dip," 2) colored glass, 3) gelatin, and 4) plastic.

Lamp dip is a special paint that you can obtain from theatrical supply houses. Its most valuable use is in painting projection slides. It is, however, also used for coloring "A," "P," or "S" lamps, usually in light tints. Since heat tends to discolor the paint, it is limited to use on lamps of 40 watts or less. It is possible to buy lamps that have been dipped, or to dip them yourself. The most common type of Christmas tree lights are usually colored in this manner. The color can wear off, but is more frequently scratched off. Normal paint cannot be used because it is not heat-resistant and will blister and fall off. This medium is used occasionally on low-wattage striplights, but it is the least desirable of all media.

Colored glass is glass in which the pigment or color was impregnated when it was made. The color goes all the way through the glass and will not come off or discolor. It is possible to obtain lamps in many sizes and shapes with colored glass bulbs. It is also possible to buy color slides, usually called "roundels," that will fit in lighting instruments or compartmentalized striplights. This is the most expensive color medium, and the color range is effective only in the darker colors. It is quite satisfactory for the three primary colors. It cuts down intensity more than some of the other media. Because of its durability, it is most desirable for use in striplights. Although more expensive, the roundels are preferable to the lamps. You can then change wattages without having to worry about color, and the roundels are permanent if not broken accidentally, whereas the lamps burn out and must be replaced.

Up until the early 1960's, gelatin was the most popular color medium. It is the least expensive material. It can be obtained in any color. It is easily cut with a pair of scissors. It is actually regular gelatin, impregnated with pigment, formed into sheets and hardened. Heat from lamps causes it to become brittle, crack, and break. Strong light causes the color to fade. If placed too close to a hot bulb, it will scorch or burn. Heat also causes it to shrink.

When you use gelatin, cut it larger than the hole in the color frame so that, when it shrinks, it will still cover the opening. Do not puncture it with pins or brass fasteners because when it gets hot and brittle, the shrinking effect requires freedom of movement or it will crack and break. Some colors fade more quickly than others, and higher intensities will cause quicker fading. For this reason it is necessary to check each instrument prior to each performance and, where necessary, replace the faded gelatin. Water or excessive moisture causes gelatin to melt.

Do not use cellophane, celluloid, or colored paper as substitutes for gelatin. They are flammable and constitute dangerous fire hazards.

Plastic was first introduced in the United States in the late 1950's. It had just been developed in England. It was not very popular at first because it cost twice as much as gelatin and was difficult to obtain because of limited import from English manufacturers. It does not fade or become brittle and therefore is much more durable than gelatin. Because of its durability it is, in the long run, less expensive than gelatin and by the 1960's had become more popular than gelatin. As a result, it is now available from theatrical suppliers, and the price, though still higher than gelatin, has decreased proportionately.

Plastic is thicker and stiffer than gelatin and will, if necessary, stand by itself without the use of a color frame. It is advisable, however, to use it in color frames wherever possible. In spite of its thickness it can be cut with scissors almost as readily as gelatin. Incidentally, it is waterproof, if by any chance you have occasion to use it where it might get wet. Remember, however, that the normal lighting instrument is not waterproof.

There is no standardized color system for theatrical lighting any more than there is in the paint industry. Each manufacturer uses his own nomenclature and numbering system to designate the colors. The most popular gelatin suppliers in the United States are Brigham Gelatin Company and Rosco Labs. The most popular plastics are Cinemoid, a British product, and Roscolene, made by Rosco Labs. Major Equipment Company, a Chicago lighting manufacturer, has put a new plastic on the market called Majeroid. Major has advertised that they will use the same nomenclature as Cinemoid. The listing below is an attempt to compare the nomenclature of these manufacturers and to recommend the most desirable use for each color. It is not a complete listing by any means. It contains the colors that you will use most frequently.

The complementary colors on lines 4 and 11 are most suitable for warm, bright acting areas and gay comedy scenes. Complementary colors on lines 6 and 12 are not quite as warm. Use them for romantic and mysterious moods. Complementary colors on lines 2 and 14 are more neutral, usable as cool areas for comedy and as warm areas for tragedy. Complementary colors on lines 5 and 11 may be used for cool, romantic, and mysterious areas. The coldest area colors are on lines 8 and 13. Use them for somber, dark, and tragic scenes. Generally, then, for light comedies use 4 & 11, 6 & 12, and 2 & 14. For romantic drama use 6 & 12, 2 & 14, and 8 & 13, and for tragedy use 2 & 14, 5 & 11, and 8 & 13. Other combinations may be used depending upon the mood you wish to set. The warmest areas should be on the side of the stage where the light is supposed to emanate (a window, fireplace, or lighting fixture). Remember, however, in order to get a realistic fireplace effect, they cast a warm, flickering light on the opposite wall. The wall above the fireplace is always relatively darker and cooler. A similar situation also occurs when warm sunlight comes through a window, except that it doesn't flicker.

Certain precautions must be kept in mind when you use color. Many things you can

LINE	ROSCOGEL	ROSCOLENE	BRIGHAM	CINEMOID (MAJEROID)	RECOMMENDED USAGE
1	201 Frost	801 Frost	1 Frost	29 Heavy Frost	to diffuse light—cut hole in center.
2	203 Dk. Bastard Amber	802 Bastard Amber	62 Lt. Scarlet	53 Pale Salmon	acting area—complement with line 14 below.
3	205 Lt. Straw	805 Lt. Straw	54 Lt. Straw	3 Straw	dull sunlight—tonal—comedy.
4	212 Pale Amber	809 Straw			bright sunlight—acting area—complement with line 11 below.
5	213 Lt. Amber			4 Med. Amber	bright sunlight—acting area—complement with line 11 below.
6	214 Med. Amber	813 Lt. Amber	57 Lt. Amber		sunlight—acting area—complement with line 12 below.
7	222 Fire Red	821 Lt. Red	67 Fire Red	6 Primary Red	primary color—tonal—dark sunset—fire—flame.
8	225 No Color Pink	825 No Color Pink	2 Lt. Flesh Pink		acting area—complement with line 13 below.
9	226 Flesh Pink	826 Flesh Pink	3 Flesh Pink		tonal—gay comedy.
10	238 Dark Magenta	838 Dark Magenta	12 Dark Magenta	12 Deep Rose	tonal—warm, rich.
11	242 Surprise Pink	841 Surprise Pink			nightlight—acting area—complement with lines 4 and 5 above.
12		842 Special Lavender	17 Special Lavender	36 Pale Lavender	nighttime—acting area—complement with line 6 above.
13	251 Daylight Blue	851 Daylight Blue	25 Daylight Blue	17 Steel Blue	cool moonlight—acting area—complement with line 8 above.
14	254 Special Steel Blue	854 Steel Blue	29 Special Steel Blue	18 Lt. Blue	bright moonlight—acting area—complement with line 2 above.
15	257 Med. Blue	857 Med. Blue	33 Med. Blue	32 Med. Blue	dark moonlight.
16	259 Green Blue	859 Green Blue	41 Moonlight Blue		moonlight effect.
17	265 Dark Blue	866 Dark Urban Blue	36 Non-fade Blue	20 Deep Blue	primary color—tonal dark sky—moonlight.
18	274 Dark Green	874 Dark Green	49 Dark Green	39 Primary Green	primary color—tonal foliage lighting.

discover only through experience and experimentation, others will save you time and expense and are worth your consideration. The first involves the use of white costumes, props, and scenery. Remember that white surfaces reflect the color of the light. A white gown will look blue if the wearer is standing in a blue light and it will turn red, green, or yellow as it is moved into each colored light beam. If the wearer is standing in an area lighted on one side by a blue light and the other by an amber light, the gown will look half blue and half yellowish-orange. On the other hand, an off-white, such as oyster, light beige, blue-white, etc., will have just enough color in it to avoid apparent reflection of the light colors and will appear, to the audience, to be a white gown.

Another area in which care must be exercised is in the use of green lights on actors' faces. It makes complexions look muddy. It blackens rouge and lipstick. It turns blond hair green, and gives redheads dark gray or black hair. It frequently will exaggerate the slightest blemish on an actor's face. In other words, keep the greens off the actors' faces. Be careful of the yellow-greens, blue-greens, and moonlight blues for the same reason. Some of them have enough green in them to cause trouble.

When using cross-area lighting, lights must be aimed with precise care, otherwise you will have places on the stage that are lighted with one color only, or with colors that are not complementary. You must take similar care to keep acting area lights off the scenery as much as possible, otherwise the shadows that they cast will have some unusual, and unexpected, colors. Avoiding unwanted shadows will be discussed further in Chapter XIV.

Some lighting designers prefer to use related colors rather than complementary colors. In such a case, you would light an area with two colors that are closely related to each other, such as Light Pink and Special Lavender or Surprise Pink and Bastard Amber. Many combinations may be chosen to suit mood, costume colors, and makeup. Remember that any two colors in one area must be related colors. This approach requires that you devote considerable study and experimentation to get the best combinations until you have acquired a lot of experience using related colors. The complementary system is preferable because it gives objects a three-dimensional appearance (called plasticity), which is lost when you use the related-color system, because of insufficient contrast. You also lose the realistic shadow effect and you have less flexibility to change mood by varying the mix of the two complementary colors.

There is also the single-color approach, which has all of the disadvantages of the related-color system and is more monotonous to the viewer. It is, therefore, not recommended. Some proponents of the single-color system suggest that, with proper side lighting and general lighting, the disadvantages may be overcome. Even the monotony may be broken up with the use of special lighting for accents. Such an approach, however, is as archaic as the use of footlights. As with footlights, it makes it very difficult and unnatural to avoid unreal, grotesque shadows. In addition, at its best it requires the use of considerably more lighting instruments, control equipment, and electrical power.

No matter which approach you use, do not allow yourself to be confined or limited by your approach. You may be able to get the effect you want by combining two, or all three, of these systems. What you must do is experiment, create, and try to develop a color system that is better than any of the others for your purpose. In doing so, remember that color and lighting are important only to the extent that they contribute to the playwright's intent and the director's approach. If your design becomes an end, or goal, within itself, it then detracts from the production and is, by any standards, poor lighting.

Chapter XIII

SPECIAL EFFECTS

The term "special effects" should bring to mind the magic and the illusion of the theatre. Of course, in all its aspects the theatre deals with illusion, but the most spectacular and magical are the special effects. The expression itself conjures up a picture of rabbits disappearing, people flying around, trains speeding across the stage, lightning crashing, and thunder rumbling in the ears of the audience.

Special effects are of several types. Some are mechanical contrivances, some are electrical, and some are electronic. A few theatrical organizations consider that all special effects are properties and the responsibility of the property manager. Others classify them as scenery, or sound effects, or lighting. In the professional theatre, anything that requires electricity to operate comes under the domain of the master electrician and his crew. The most common approach to classification, even in the professional theatre, is that all special effects that create a noise are sound effects. All that are used for the purpose of transmitting light are lighting effects, and all others come under the category of properties or stagecraft. We are primarily concerned with special lighting effects under the last mentioned classification.

In Chapter V we discussed the types of projection instruments that are used for special effects. Projection instruments are the most common source of lighting effects. Figure 55 shows a scenic effect that was produced with a stereopticon. In this case, the Seal of England was projected on a background above the Queen's head for a symbolic, scenic effect. It is even possible to use projectors on white backdrops and backings to project scenery. Although the idea has limitations, it certainly makes scene changes quick and easy. The main concern of this chapter, however, will be to describe the means of obtaining the effects that you will be required to use most often, such as fireplace light, lightning, sunlight, moonlight, etc.

The effect that is probably used most frequently is that of an open fire, usually in a fireplace, but possibly in a campfire upon occasion. If it is a log fire, real logs are not recommended because there is no way to make them look as though they are burning. Your property manager should furnish "logs" made of papier-mâché or similar material. They should be shaped and painted to look as though they are burning. The best color paints to use are flame red, oranges, and ambers. Glowing ashes can be made in a similar manner; and, of course, if it is a coal fire, coal-shaped papier-mâché is used instead of the log-shaped pieces.

You obtain the glow by locating an "A," "P," or "S" lamp (60 watts) out of sight behind the logs. The lamp should be colored red, using any of the media described in the previous chapter. If the flames are to be visible to the audience, place a small, silent

94 / Practical Stage Lighting

Figure 55

electric fan behind or under the logs or coals. Direct the fan so that the airflow is straight upward. Fasten small strips of lightweight red and orange cloth, or tissue paper, to the grill of the fan so that they blow freely when the fan is on. You will probably need a lamp with a higher wattage. In any case, make sure that it is placed in the best position to reflect the light from, or through, the blowing strips of material.

If you wish to get the effect of flames reflecting on the scenery or the actors' faces, use a spotlight with the proper color. Place the fan below the light so that the strips of material are blown up in front of the lens. From that position, direct the light on the object that is to be bathed in firelight. You will find that variegated revolving lights are available from theatrical supply houses. They will usually create whatever firelight effect you want.

Many devices will produce the effect of lightning. White light is generally used and, therefore, the simplest means is to flick your stage worklights on and off quickly. This is not only the simplest, but frequently the most effective, lightning, especially for outdoor scenes. If you have a ceiling on your setting, the worklights may work fairly well for indoor scenes. The pitfall is when you have lightning indoors without any flash outside through the windows. In many cases, you may want the effect to appear only through the windows or doorways. The same color principle applies. Place a 75- or 100-watt lamp out of sight, behind the door or window flat. If it is not bright enough, use two or more lamps. Do not use lamps that exceed 100 watts since their afterglow, as the filament cools down, will spoil the effect. Paint the back of the window and door flats with a dark color so the light will not shine through the scenery. If you have a free, uncolored circuit in your borderlights, or cyclorama striplights, you can use that to obtain a very effective bright flash of lightning.

Chain lightning is more difficult. Years ago, stage electricians would actually create a flash of lightning by shorting out a live electrical circuit between a piece of iron and a carbon rod. This is hazardous, and most safety regulations prohibit it. If the technical director does not object, cut a lightning-shaped opening in the backing or backdrop and flick a 75- or 100-watt lamp behind the opening. It is necessary to paint the back of the scenery black to keep the light from shining through the uncut portion. Since this is a sure way of ruining the scenery for future use, you may not be allowed to use this method. An alternate method is to use a projector with a lightning-shaped slide. Direct it at the spot on the scenery where the flash is to appear. Do not turn it on and off. Use an opaque mask in front of the lens; turn the projector on at least 10 seconds before you need it; then, flick the mask down and back up in front of the lens quickly. Then turn it off. The downward first movement is important to have the lightning appear from the normal direction whence a lightning flash originates. You can also obtain special lightning devices from theatrical supply houses. They may or may not be more effective for your particular application.

Another effect that you will need to create frequently is sunlight. Sunlight streaming through a window or doorway, in an interior setting, is no problem. A beam projector, using the right color, is very effective. It should be higher than the top of the opening and shining in from offstage, where the audience cannot see the instrument. If you don't have a beam projector, you can use a 750- or 1,000-watt spotlight for a convincing effect. Focus the beam so that it is larger than the opening in the scenery. When you shine any light on scenery from offstage, you must paint the back of the scenery with a dark color, preferably black, to keep the light from shining through the canvas.

Outdoor sunlight is more difficult, unless you have enough beam projectors to flood the stage from one side. You can use a few large (750- to 1,000-watt) scoops effectively. In any case, your tonal and general lighting will be almost as bright as your acting area lighting, but it should emanate from the warm side of the stage only. Yellow-green colors are effective to simulate sunlight through foliage realistically, but you must be aware of their effect upon the actors' faces.

Everything above that pertains to sunlight also applies to moonlight, except the colors. If you have a nighttime scene indoors, with or without moonlight, it is not enough to turn the sunlight off outside the windows. In order to obtain a convincing nighttime effect, it is necessary to use a blue light shining in the windows. The shade of blue will depend upon how dark the night is and what mood you wish to establish.

Outdoor moonlight is easier than sunlight, since it need not be anywhere near as bright. Otherwise, the same principle applies. In any outdoor nighttime scene, the acting areas should be lighted primarily with suitable nighttime shades of blue. If you need warm colors, a source of warm light must be established, such as a campfire, street light, house window, or even moonlight, although, realistically, the moon casts a cool, not a warm, beam.

You will have many occasions to use, on the stage, floor lamps, table lamps, chandeliers, and wall candelabra. Most of the time you will find that these fixtures need to be lighted. Running a light cable to the fixture to hook it up is usually no problem. The problem lies in the effect that the light will have on your stage lighting picture. First of all, a bare lamp shining in the audience's eyes is distracting and sometimes blinding. Secondly, a lamp of 15 watts or more can cast shadows and harsh white light in the wrong places. The answer to this problem is to keep a few 7½-watt lamps with frosted bulbs on hand and when you use a household fixture, replace its lamp with one of the 7½-watt lamps. You can usually obtain them from any electrical supply dealer. They are made with both medium and candelabra screw bases and can frequently be found in other sizes and shapes. You may also obtain "flicker" lamps that automatically flash on and off to give a candle or open-flame effect. You can get a realistic effect with them, especially if you can shade them from the audience's direct view.

We have covered the special effects that you will be required to create most frequently. Before we leave the subject, something should be said about transparencies. They are becoming more and more popular in school and community theatres. They can be used very effectively in Children's Theatre. A transparency is a fabric, commonly called a "scrim," which is woven in a very loose, netlike weave. It looks like a woman's veil or cheesecloth, although a good scrim should be stronger than a veil or cheesecloth. If you wish more information concerning the qualities of scrim, please refer to a book of stagecraft. Why, then, are we talking about transparencies in a book on lighting? Because the proper utilization of a scrim depends solely on the use of your lights in relation to the scrim. A book on lighting would be incomplete if it didn't tell you how to light transparencies. When a scrim is hung on the stage, stretched to a smooth surface, and illumined from the front only, it appears to be a solid, opaque wall or curtain. If you then turn on a light behind the scrim to light an object that is behind the scrim, the object appears to the audience to materialize from out of nowhere and to have an eerie quality about it. If you then turn off the lights that are shining on the front of the scrim and light the area behind the scrim, the audience will not see the scrim at all. The "opaque wall" will seem to disappear. You can also use a scrim as a backdrop or cyclorama, as long as you use no lights behind it. In addition, you can project a scene on a scrim. You may place the projector in front of, or behind, the scrim and you will get the same image on the transparency. In Figure 55, the blue background is a scrim. In this case it is lighted from the front with blue striplights and scoops.

We have barely scratched the surface of a list of all possible special lighting effects. Unfortunately, it would take a lot of space to discuss every effect. Most of the remaining ones are seldom used. It would be a waste of our time to try to list them all. The secret of successful special effects is the use of imagination and ingenuity. For instance, a plain kitchen globe-type ceiling lighting fixture, hung sideways, became a most realistic moon when it was turned on behind a blue-lighted scrim. A spotlight reflecting from a shallow pan of shimmering water didn't give a very realistic effect of light reflected from the surface of a lake until both the pan and the spotlight were vibrated. Finally, do not forget the effects that may be obtained with the use of "black light," which we discussed in Chapter V. The possibilities are limitless. One lighting designer is proud of his motto, "If they can't do it any other way, we can always do it with lights." Very likely he has been stumped on occasion, but it's a good attitude because it serves as a challenge to himself to look constantly for new and unusual ways to create special lighting effects.

Chapter XIV

LIGHTING THE PROSCENIUM STAGE

Like the Walrus in *Alice Through the Looking-Glass,* we have talked of many things. In our case, it has been electricity, tools, lamps and lenses, reflectors, instruments, colors, and controls. We have now reached the point that we can put these things together and see how to light the stage. The basics you need to start to light your stage are answers to the following questions: Where do I put my lights? What types of lights do I use? How strong should they be?

The answers to the above questions vary depending upon the size and type of theatre. For the sake of clarity, let us confine ourselves, in this chapter, to the proscenium type of stage. The common practice is to divide the acting area of the stage into nine areas as shown in Figure 56. On wider stages, it may be expanded to as many as fifteen areas. Regardless of dimensions, you will be required to light the downstage, midstage, and upstage areas.

You will illuminate the downstage areas with lights that are suspended on the "house pipe," sometimes referred to as the "apron pipe" or "AP" lights. These lights are set over the audience's head, as close to the stage as possible, so that their beams form a 60° angle to the horizontal at the eye level of an actor standing in the downstage areas. Figure 57 illustrates the way you should use a protractor to measure the vertical angle in order to place your lights properly. Incidentally, you should place all acting area lights in positions that result in the same vertical angle of light, regardless of which acting areas they hit. By doing this, your lights will cast more natural light than they would at any other angle. Both sunlight and indoor ceiling lights emanate from the same approximate angle in more cases than from any other one angle. The resultant shadows are not likely to hit the scenery, and yet the light is not so high as to cast grotesque face shadows on normal facial features.

Once you have established the height of the pipe, you will want to know where, on the pipe, to place each of your instruments, in other words, the horizontal angle. Since you should use the cross-area lighting system, you will be utilizing two lights for each acting area. They should be placed equidistant from the area that they are to hit, so that their beams intersect each other at a 60° angle as illustrated in Figure 58.

You may be wondering how far away from each area the lights should be placed. It is not wise to set specific distances for various wattages of spotlights. Too many other factors must be considered. The brightness of the area to be lighted is chiefly determined by the wattage of the lamp in relation to the distance that the light beam travels. It can vary considerably, however, depending on the efficiency of the lighting instrument, the width of the beam, the amount of light that is absorbed by the materials that it hits, and

98 / Practical Stage Lighting

```
| UP RIGHT (UR) | UP CENTER (UC) | UP LEFT (UL) |
| RIGHT (R)     | CENTER (C)     | LEFT (L)     |
| DOWN RIGHT (DR) | DOWN CENTER (DC) | DOWN LEFT (DL) |
```

Figure 56

the color media. The distance of the farthest row of seats is also important, because the farther the viewer must see, the brighter the stage must be. Under average conditions, however, the following wattages should be adequate.

Distance beam travels	Spotlight wattage
15' to 19'	250 watts
20' to 24'	500 watts
25' to 29'	750 watts
30' to 39'	1,000 watts
40' to 49'	1,500 watts
50' or more	2,000 watts

The above information should be sufficient to plan the use of your instruments. Most spotlights are rated 250 to 500 watts, 500 to 750 watts, 750 to 1,000 watts, and so forth. Plan to use an instrument that is rated to the higher level. Then if it is not bright enough you need only change lamps to the higher wattage.

The specific location of each acting area

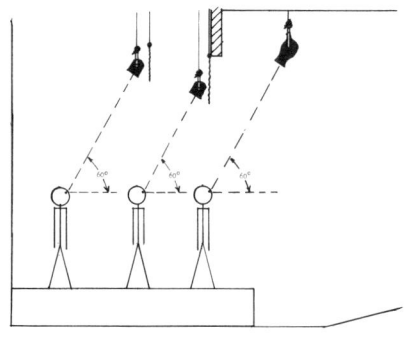

Figure 57

will be determined by the director, the confines of the scenery, and the placement of furniture and props. The size of each area will also be affected by those same factors as well as the size of the stage. You should make sure that your director knows that the larger the area, the wider you will have to focus your light beam, thereby decreasing the intensity. If the light is too dim, you will have to use an instrument with a higher wattage.

Under average conditions, the diameter of the beam when it reaches the acting area may vary from 4' to 8'. There will be occasions when you will have to provide an area as broad as 12' in diameter. You will, in such instances, need higher-wattage instruments than those recommended above.

Since the size of the stage is frequently a determining factor in setting the size of acting areas, the following chart can be used as a guideline to determine the number of acting areas that you can efficiently light under normal conditions.

Width of proscenium opening	Depth of acting area	Number of acting areas
12' to 24'	8' to 16'	six
12' to 24'	12' to 24'	nine
16' to 32'	12' to 24'	twelve
20' to 40'	12' to 24'	fifteen

Notice that there is considerable overlap to allow flexibility in the number of areas that may be used on an average-size stage. For example, if your stage has a proscenium opening of 24' and a depth of 20', you can

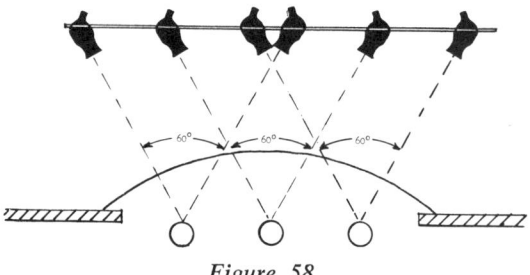

Figure 58

Lighting the Proscenium Stage / 99

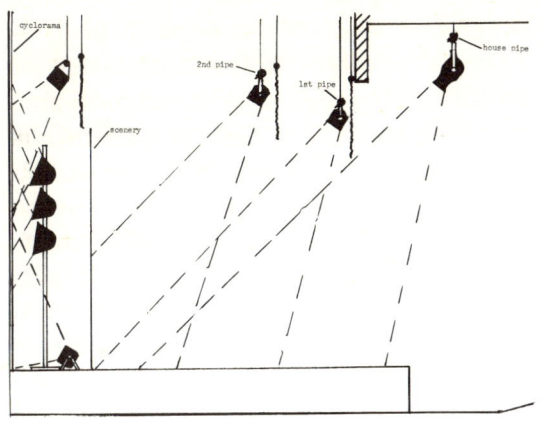

Figure 59

easily use either nine, twelve, or fifteen acting areas.

In order to light the midstage areas, you will need a pipe batten that is hung upstage of the teaser, or act curtain, as shown in Figure 59. This pipe is referred to as the "first pipe." You will light the upstage acting areas from the "second pipe," situated behind a border strip upstage of the first pipe as shown, also, in Figure 59. If you use a ceiling, you may have to place the second pipe farther downstage, or even directly above the first pipe. In doing this, you will lose the 60° vertical angle and will have to be very careful to avoid shadows on your upstage wall. Otherwise, the first and second pipes and their lights are placed by following the same rules that are set forth for the house pipe. The wattages of the instruments would, similarly, be determined by the distance the beam travels.

Figure 59 also shows the placement of cyclorama lights, both from below and from overhead. Although they are shown as striplights in the diagram, scoops are equally usable, as well as a combination of both. Figure 60, which is a top view of a lighting setup, shows both striplights and scoops being used as cyclorama lights. The striplights should be 5′ or 6′ from the cyclorama, although, if space is limited, you can place them as close as 3′. You should direct them so they cover as much of the cyclorama surface as possible. You may use 250- or 500-watt scoops for most cycloramas. The best coverage can be obtained with 500-watt scoops at about 15′, or 250-watt scoops at about 8′, from the cyclorama. Again, if you are cramped for space, you can place them as close as 3′ to 6′.

Figure 60 also shows the location of backing lights outside the doorways and window. You may hang such lights on an overhead batten, if one happens to be suitably situated. More frequently, however, you will attach them to the scenery or use pipe stands. You may use low-wattage scoops or small, 3′ striplights for this purpose. You will frequently need to use spotlights for such purposes as lighting actors' faces as they ascend stairways, emphasizing an important doorway, firelight, and acting areas on high platforms and balconies; and/or beam projectors for sunlight or moonlight streaming through a window or doorway.

It has been stated previously that you should try to keep your acting area lights off the scenery to avoid distracting shadows. The scenery, or lighting, designer, however, may request tonal, or accent, lighting to be directed upon the scenery. You will notice that Figure 60 shows striplights on both the first and second pipe. You use these primarily as tonal lighting for the acting areas. They may be directed, also, on nearby scenery to meet the designer's requirements. Try

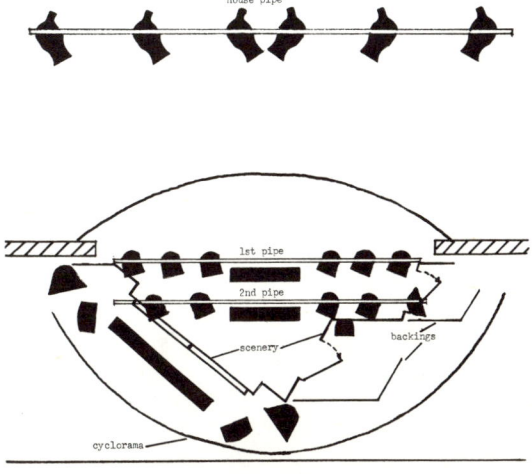

Figure 60

to keep them off the upstage wall, however, since that is where they may cast unwanted shadows. If you wish to use tonal lighting on the upstage wall, hang your striplights, or floodlights, depending upon the height of the scenery, approximately 6′ to 10′ downstage of the scenery and direct them so that they will light as much of the lower surface as possible. Be careful that they are not too bright. A good general rule to follow is that the total wattage of your tonal scenery lights on the upstage wall should not exceed one and one-half times the wattage of any one of the acting area spotlights that you are using in your adjacent, upstage acting areas. For example, if you are lighting the upstage acting areas with 500-watt spotlights, the wattage of the three scoops you are using on the back wall should not exceed 250 watts each, or a total of 750 watts. Again, like most rules, this may not apply in every case. Always experiment until you get the effect you want; but remember, if it is too bright it will draw the audience's attention when they should be watching the play, not the scenery. Remember, also, that the upper regions of the walls should always be darker than the lower regions.

In some cases you may use tormentor lights. These are lights that are attached to vertical pipes on each side of the stage, upstage of the act curtain. Tormentor lights are not used very frequently nowadays, but they can be effective when it is necessary to flood the stage with general lighting, especially in outdoor scenes. Try to keep them at least 7′ above the stage floor to avoid the footlight effect. Even then, you will have to be extremely careful to avoid unwanted shadows on both the side and the back walls of the scenery.

You may have occasion to use a follow spot. There seems to be an unwritten rule that follow spots must be located behind the audience. Most of them are, because there is usually no other suitable place. The important rule is to put the follow spot as high as you can get it and still be able to operate it. Try to get the 60° vertical angle recommended previously. If you are lucky enough to have a catwalk for your house pipe, operate your follow spot from up there. Furthermore, it is better to have two follow spots from opposite sides of the theatre, in order to get the cross-area effect. You may have noticed that most large professional theatres that use follow spots generally use two simultaneously. Whoever operates the follow spots will find that it is great fun learning to synchronize with the other operator so that you both move as though they were a single spotlight. Two good spotlight operators, after a little practice, can make it look as though the two lights were being run by one person. If you have an intercommunication system, it helps to use headphones so that you can talk to each other, but it is not necessary.

It is usually advantageous to light the act curtain between scenes and for a few seconds before the beginning of each act. This helps to set, or maintain, a mood. You may hang your curtain lights on the house pipe. Sometimes it is possible to use some of the regular acting area lights as curtain lights also. If you have footlights, you can frequently get interesting effects by using them as curtain lights. This can be especially effective if you have colors in the footlights and can change the colors by controlling their intensity from your control board. Many motion picture theatres have overhead, tormentor, and foot striplights that are used solely to light the curtain.

Chapter XV

ARENA AND THRUST STAGE LIGHTING

The previous chapter set forth the most appropriate lighting systems for the proscenium theatre. In the past twenty-five years there has been considerable experimentation with other types of theatre. Two of these, the arena theatre and the thrust stage, have flourished and are continuing to grow in popularity. Whereas the audience sees the proscenium play from only one side, they view the thrust stage from three sides and the arena stage from all sides. Therefore, in the two latter types of staging, we have the problem of lighting the stage from several angles that did not concern us in the case of the proscenium stage.

There is no question but that we must use different techniques to light the arena and thrust stages. It does not mean, however, that we must necessarily reject our philosophy of theatrical lighting. A number of designers have used the need for different techniques as an excuse to discard the old philosophy. Unfortunately, it is not clear whether a new philosophy, or any philosophy, has been offered to support the new techniques. Nevertheless, let us take a look at the new technique.

The approach to lighting arena and thrust staging is called the "water-tower" approach, because it is based upon the principle of illuminating a spherical water tower. If you refer to Figure 61, you will see how three lights may be placed equidistant from one another around a circular object, like a water tower, and their beams will illuminate the surface of the object on all sides. This proves that it is possible to light an actor completely with three lighting instruments so that his face will be illuminated at all times regardless of the direction in which he faces.

The next step is to divide the arena or thrust stage into acting areas. With the audience on three or four sides, you no longer have an upstage or downstage, or a right or left stage. What some designers have done, therefore, is to establish the center area and to surround it with a perimeter of areas, numbered clockwise, such as twelve o'clock, three o'clock, six o'clock and nine o'clock. Figure 62 diagrams a stage that has been divided in this manner. By lighting each acting area with three spotlights, you have achieved the major purpose of stage lighting. The actors are visible to each member of the audience.

If you have been paying attention to the earlier chapters, you may be able to figure out the next question. It is, "How about color?" Did you think of it yourself? Actually, the color for each area is chosen by the director and the designer based upon the mood, emphasis, and picturization that they wish to achieve in each acting area. All three lights hitting that area contain the selected color. In this way, every member of

102 / Practical Stage Lighting

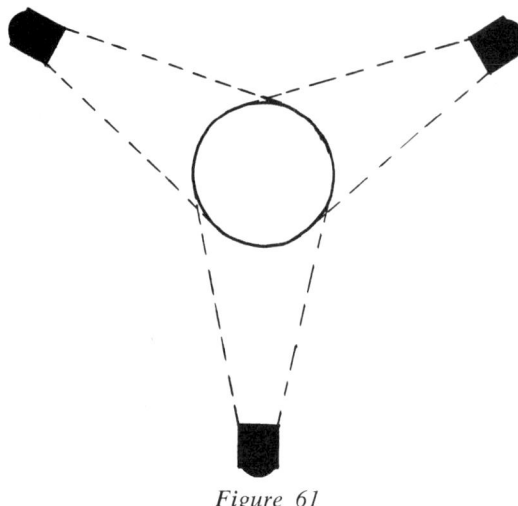

Figure 61

the audience sees the same color in each area. Figure 63 illustrates how this system is planned on paper.

This approach takes theatrical lighting back almost to the gas-illumination days. Instead of the natural-looking, 60° horizontal angle, the three light beams intersect one another at 120° angles. This, in effect, is similar to a single light hitting an actor's face from dead front and washing out most of the natural shadows. Cross-area lighting is forgotten. It is comparable to the general footlight and borderlight approaches that were discarded in proscenium staging forty years ago.

In addition, if an actor does happen to stand in one of the three positions where two of the lights will illuminate him equally and simultaneously, both are the same color and there will still be no shadow effect upon his face. There is no motivation for a natural source of light, unless the director selects all areas on one side of the stage to be warm areas and on the other side to be cool areas. That, incidentally, is poor arena and thrust staging because it results in an imbalance of color on the stage.

We could dwell upon this subject longer, but to do so would only delay the presentation of the solution to these problems. First of all, since we do not, as yet, have a better philosophy, let us go back to the cross-area approach to lighting. To make it easier to use the technique, we will use a different system to designate stage areas. Of course, center stage will always be called center stage. Let us identify the remaining areas by compass points; namely, North, Northeast, East, Southeast, South, etc. Figure 64 diagrams an arena stage divided into acting areas in this manner. Notice that it does not matter whether the stage is circular, square, or rectangular. One stipulation is that the four theatre aisles that are usually used in arena theatres intersect the stage at the Northeast, Southeast, Southwest, and Northwest areas. In this way, the four arena audiences, as defined and separated by the aisles, will be seated facing either the North, South, East, or West acting areas. In the thrust theatre, they would be facing any three of the four areas.

The director and the designer must select two diagonally opposite acting areas to be the warmest areas, and the other two corner areas will then be the coldest. In this way each member of the audience will have a cold area on one side of him and a warm area on the other side, as shown in Figure 65.

With this in mind, you assign four lights to each acting area, two warm and two cool.

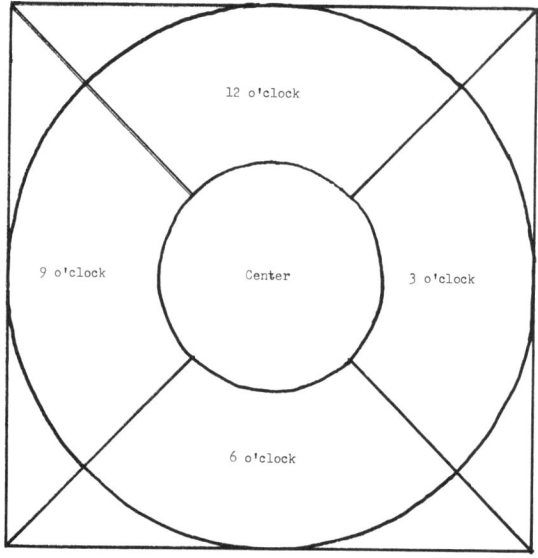

Figure 62

Arena and Thrust Stage Lighting / 103

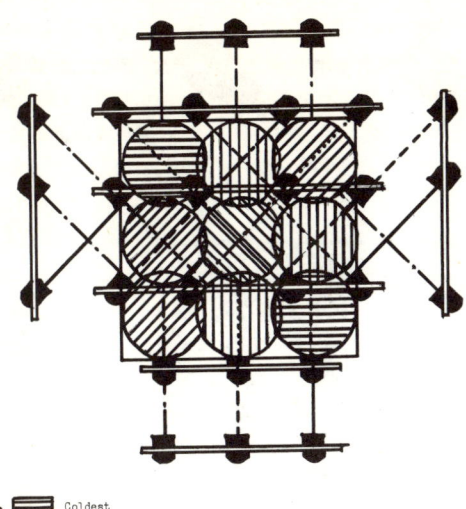

Figure 63

The warm lights will emanate from the two warm directions and the cool lights will emanate from the cool sides. The closer to the warm corners an area is, the warmer the complementary color mix you use. As the areas approach the cold corners, you use the cooler complementary color combinations.

As you can see in Figure 65, the beams from each of the four lights in a given area intersect one another at 90° angles. Although it is not as desirable as the ideal 60° horizontal angle, the 90° angle will give realistic-looking shadows and will enhance the facial features, rather than washing them out. Of course, if you have enough instruments, you can use two on each side that intersect at 60°. It would require eight lights for each area, twice as many.

Even with four instruments for each area, the only disadvantage to the cross-area technique is that it requires more lighting instruments. This was true, also, when it was first introduced to the proscenium stage. If you use nine acting areas, the "water-tower" approach requires the use of twenty-seven acting area spotlights, whereas cross-area technique requires thirty-six acting area spotlights. If you use tonal lighting, the number of instruments would be the same regardless of which system you used. The water-tower approach is excellent for tonal lighting, so you would have your tonal lights emanate from three directions only, even with cross-area, acting area lighting. This is shown in Figure 65.

Regardless of which technique you use, a major problem in arena and thrust lighting is keeping the lights from shining into the audience's eyes on the opposite side of the stage. It is here that the 60° vertical angle becomes important. You must use it. In some cases you may have to use an even higher angle.

In arena and thrust staging, the actors make many, if not all, entrances and exits through the theatre aisles. In many cases the director may require that their faces be lighted as they are going up or down an aisle. You should ask your director to avoid this wherever possible. In many instances, however, it will be necessary. You can do it with an ellipsoidal spotlight aimed up the aisle from above the stage for entrances and aimed down the aisle from the back of the theatre for exits. These lights must be shuttered so that the light beam hits the aisle space only, and not the audience sitting on either side of the aisle. Try to maintain the 60°

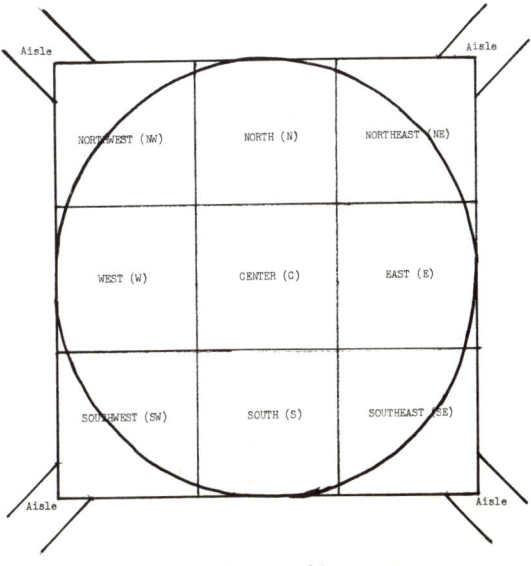

Figure 64

104 / Practical Stage Lighting

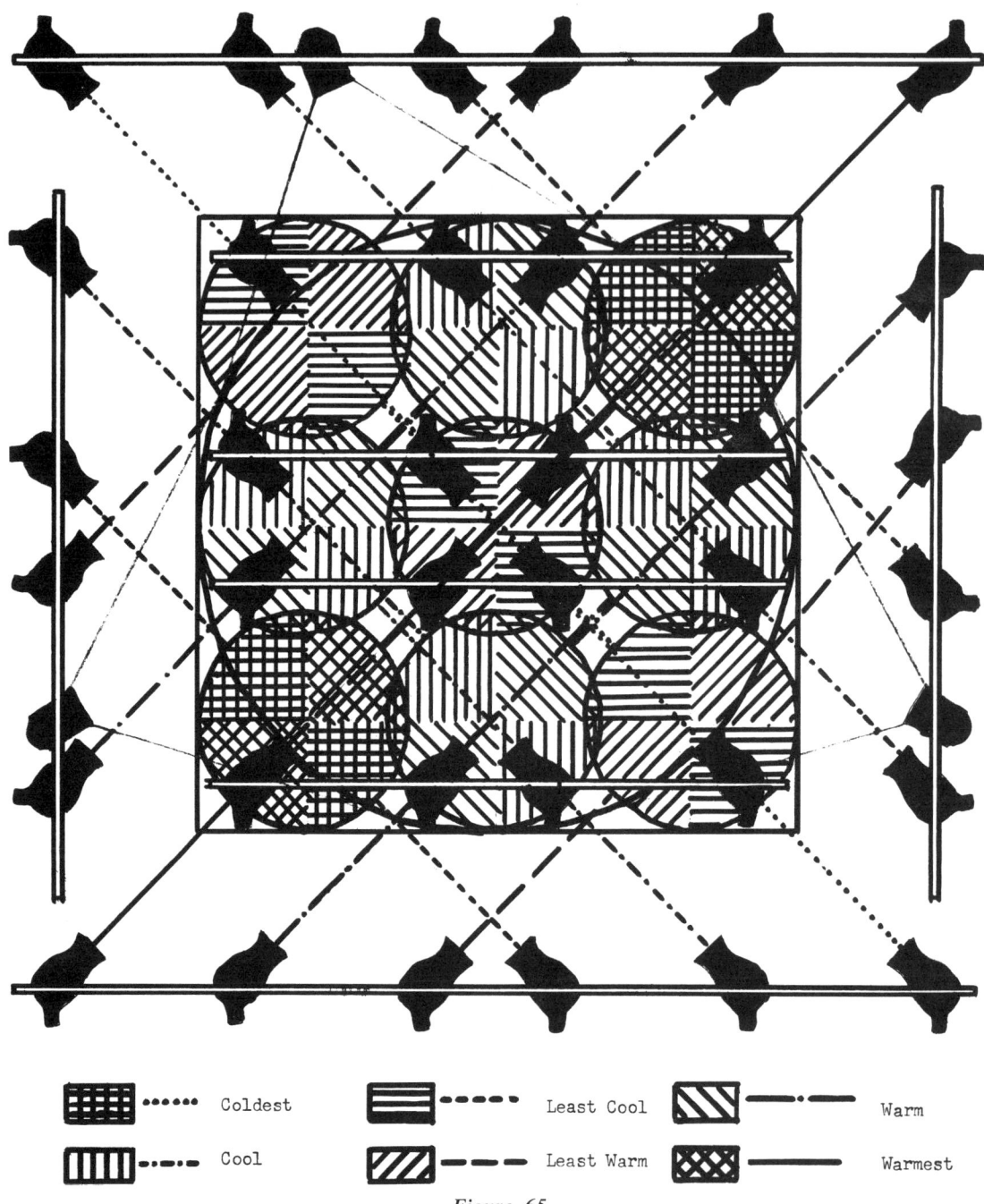

Figure 65

vertical angle even if it makes it necessary to use more lighting instruments, each one hitting a portion of the aisle.

It is recommended that you use only spotlights on arena stages. Striplights have a limited use on thrust stages. Both striplights and floodlights throw widely dispersed light rays that cannot be kept out of the audience's eyes. On thrust stages, striplights may be used for tonal lighting, but they must be directed from the side that is opposite the nonaudience side so that they shine toward the back wall of the stage. In all cases, for tonal lighting, you can cover an area broad enough for the average arena or thrust stage with widely focused Fresnel spots. You can keep the light from the Fresnels from annoying the audience by using stovepipes or side masks (barn-doors) to shield the beams from the audience. They are accessories that fit on the front of the instrument and act as shutters. You may adjust them to shield or narrow the beam.

A theatre designed for arena or thrust staging will usually have adequate provisions to hang your lighting instruments on overhead pipes. Frequently, however, these stages are erected in ballrooms or other large rooms that contain no suitable structural supports on which you can mount your lights. In such cases you can obtain adequate lighting by using four large pipe stands, 14' to 18' high, with cross arms at the top. Place one of these at each corner of the stage. You can mount your lights on the cross arms and the upper portions of the pipe stand. You may clamp as many as eight or nine instruments on each stand.

Another system that has been used successfully is to connect the tops of the four stands together with cross pipes each of which parallels one side of the stage. This arrangement is not safe if the distance between pipe stands exceeds 15', unless you are able to support the cross pipes from the ceiling as well. The cross pipe must be at least 1" nominal inside diameter (I.D.).

Chapter XVI

LIGHTING PLOTS AND CUE SHEETS

Planning is an essential factor in the lighting technician's job. Whether you do the planning yourself or carry out the plans that have been formulated by someone else, you still must be familiar with the tools and systems that are used to convey the plans and ideas to other people. They are usually conveyed by means of paperwork, and the systems used have been standardized so that the other people can understand them.

Two major classifications of documents are used for stage lighting. They are "lighting plots" and "cue sheets." The lighting plots are the documents used to describe the designer's plans so that the lighting instruments can be set in accordance with those plans. The cue sheets are the documents used to tell the control board operator what he is to do and when he is to do it, in order to have the stage properly lighted at all times during the progress of the production. The lighting plot tells you how to set a show, the cue sheet tells you how to run a show.

The lighting plot consists of two parts, which may be separate documents, or both part of one document. One is the lighting floor plan, which shows the location and use of all lighting instruments that will be required for each scene during the play. Frequently there is a separate floor plan for each scene and, sometimes an overall floor plan showing all lights in the theatre. In devising a floor plan, it is common practice to use symbols to represent each type of lighting instrument. Figure 66 shows the standard symbols that we use. Templates for tracing these symbols are available from lighting manufacturers and most theatrical supply houses.

Using these symbols, you can make a floor plan like the example shown in Figure 67. The floor plan alone cannot give sufficient information describing the wattage, color, size, and area of each light. In order to convey all of the design information, the floor plan must be accompanied by an instrument schedule as shown in Figure 68. You will note that it lists every instrument, indicating its type, size, wattage, lamp type, color, area, and identification number. The floor plan, along with the instrument schedule, gives you your lighting plot containing the complete design of the lighting for a given production.

At this point you are probably wondering how one goes about making up a floor plan. What is involved? As in most jobs, the only way to find out is to try it. With that in mind, let us devise a lighting plot for an actual production. Assume that your theatre is going to produce *Peer Gynt* by Henrik Ibsen. The first thing you must do is read the play. The version that has been chosen is the one produced by the American National Theatre and Academy, adapted by Paul Green. It is published by Samuel French Inc., 25 West 45th Street, New York, N.Y. 10036.

After you read the play, you attend the

first production meeting with the director, scene designer, and costumer. You are given the following information:

1) Wing and drop settings will be used.
2) To minimize scene changes, the drop will be a transparency upon which slides will be projected from the rear, and in some scenes the scrim will be lighted from the front for background, mood lighting.
3) The wings will be interchangeable.

That is, they will have Norwegian pines and rocks painted on one fold, and desert palms and sand dunes on the other fold. In this manner, a change from Norway to the African scenes may be effected by reversing the wings and changing the projection slides on the scrim.

4) The predominant scenery colors for the Norwegian scenes are deep blues, gray-blues, and deep greens. The costumes are mostly bright, warm colors,

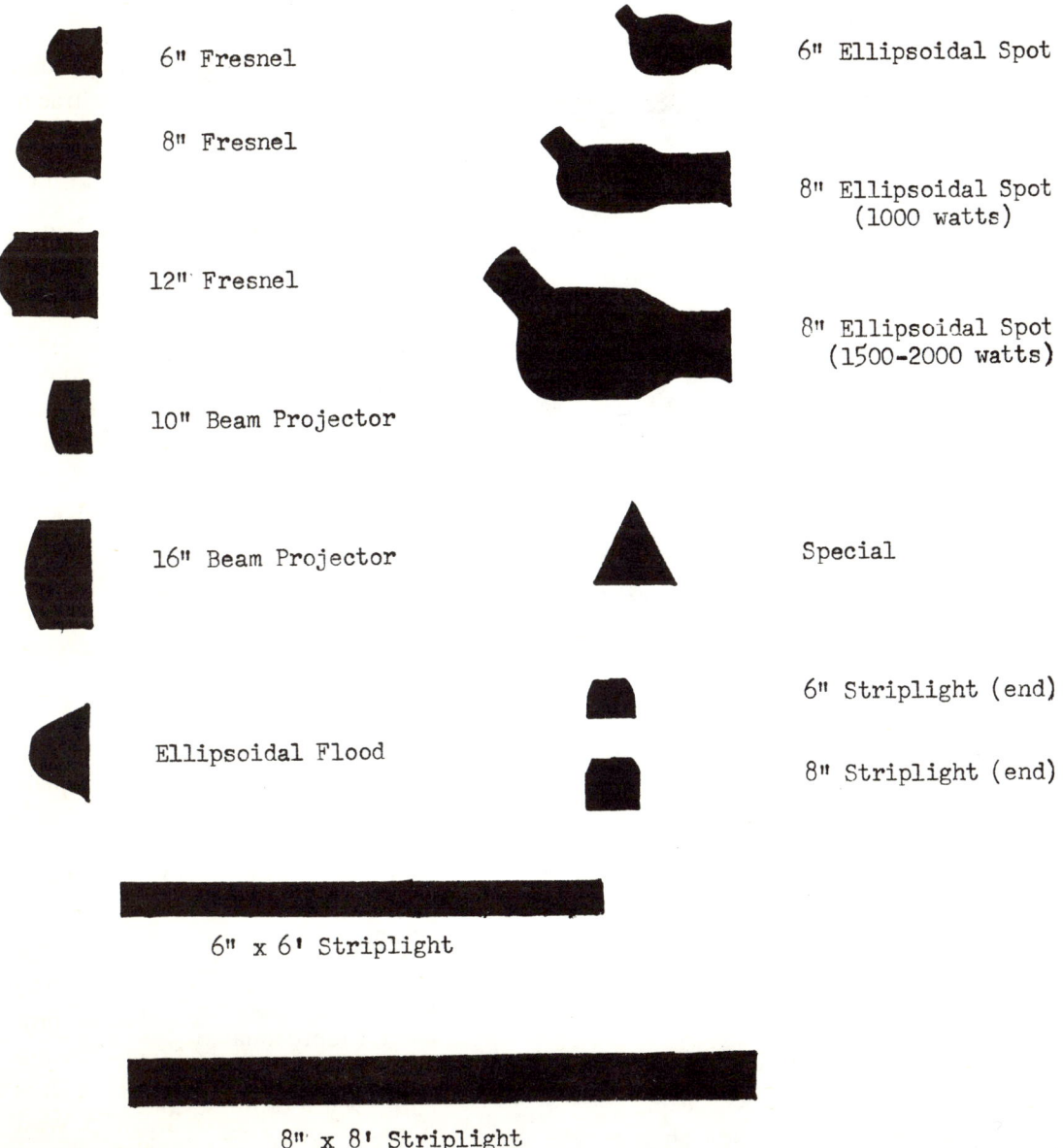

Figure 66

108 / Practical Stage Lighting

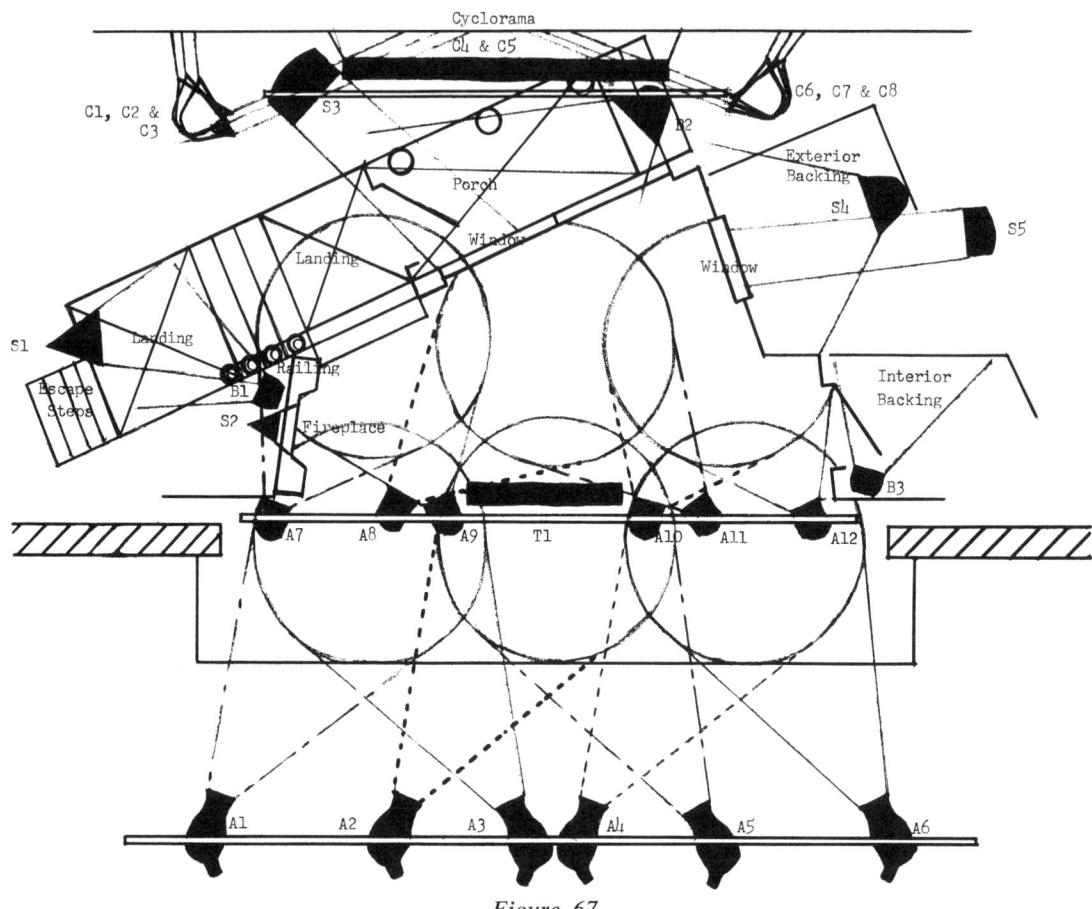

Figure 67

except for the Troll scene in which they will be earthy browns and greens. The predominant scenery colors in the African scenes are tans, browns, light blues, and light greens. The costumes will be pastels, metallics, and light-colored men's business suits.

5) A platform 36" high will be used in three areas, namely UR, UL, and behind the scrim (for the apparition scenes). The platform is designed to look like a large rock.

6) The director plans to use nine acting areas; three upstage, three midstage, and three downstage.

7) The stage is 30' wide at the proscenium opening and 25' deep.

8) The play will be taken on tour to a few high schools whose stage dimensions, at this time, are unknown.

As an experienced lighting designer, you immediately advise the director as follows:

1) The upstage areas will be difficult to light because the area lighting will wash out the colors and projections on the transparency. In fact, the upstage platforms cannot be lighted without ruining the effects on the scrim.

2) The scrim should be located no farther than 15' upstage to allow sufficient (approximately 10') throw for the Linnebach projector to cover the entire width of the scrim.

3) A black floorcloth should be used to

Lighting Plots and Cue Sheets / 109

minimize other washout on the scrim because of light reflecting from the floor.

The director tells you that, if you can light the apron, he can get along with the downstage and midstage areas, except for UC, which he needs during the Troll scene, and UR for the Wedding scene and Mountain Hut scene. The scenery designer notes that there will be scenery UR in front of the scrim during the Wedding and Mountain Hut scenes. These will shield the scrim from the area lighting and solve the washout problem. You advise the director that you will find some method of lighting the UC area for the Troll scene, but you are still concerned about the UR and UL platform areas. The director agrees to move the platforms downstage to the R and L areas. He states, however, that since he is moving the action of the play downstage, he will need a total of twelve acting areas instead of the previously stated nine. These are DR, DRC, DC, DLC, DL, R, RC, C, LC, L, UR, and UC. Both the director and the scene designer agree upon the use of a black floorcloth, and the initial planning meeting is over.

Now you must list and organize your problem areas as follows:

1) Where to place your twenty-four spot-

Light #	Type	Watts	Lamp #	Color	Area	Pipe	Dimmer #	Purpose
				INSTRUMENT SCHEDULE				
A-1	Leko	750	T12	Lt. Amber	DR	House	B3	acting area - warm
A-2	Leko	750	T12	Bast. Amber	DC	House	B2	acting area - neutral
A-3	Leko	750	T12	Spec. Lavendr.	DR	House	B3	acting area - warm
A-4	Leko	750	T12	No Color Pink	DL	House	B1	acting area - cool
A-5	Leko	750	T12	Steel Blue	DC	House	B2	acting area - neutral
A-6	Leko	750	T12	Daylight Blue	DL	House	B1	acting area - cool
A-7	Fresnel	500	T20	Lt. Amber	R	1st	A3	acting area - warm
A-8	Fresnel	500	T20	Bast. Amber	C	1st	A2	acting area - neutral
A-9	Fresnel	500	T20	Spec. Lavendr.	R	1st	A3	acting area - warm
A10	Fresnel	500	T20	No Color Pink	L	1st	A1	acting area - cool
A11	Fresnel	500	T20	Steel Blue	C	1st	A2	acting area - neutral
A12	Fresnel	500	T20	Daylight Blue	L	1st	A1	acting area - cool
C-1	Scoop	500	IF	Light Red	Cyclorama		C1	paint cyke
C-2	Scoop	500	IF	Dk. Urban Blue	Cyclorama		C2	paint cyke
C-3	Scoop	500	IF	Dark Green	Cyclorama		C3	paint cyke
C-4	Strip	250	A60	Red	Cyclorama		C1	paint cyke from overhead
		250	A60	Green	Cyclorama		C3	paint cyke from overhead
		250	A60	Blue	Cyclorama		C2	paint cyke from overhead
C-5	Strip	250	A60	Red	Cyclorama		C1	paint cyke from foots
		250	A60	Green	Cyclorama		C3	paint cyke from foots
		250	A60	Blue	Cyclorama		C2	paint cyke from foots
C-6	Scoop	500	IF	Light Red	Cyclorama		C1	paint cyke
C-7	Scoop	500	IF	Dk. Urban Blue	Cyclorama		C2	paint cyke
C-8	Scoop	500	IF	Dark Green	Cyclorama		C3	paint cyke
S-1	Fresnel	500	T20	Flesh Pink	Special		B4	light faces on stairway
S-2	Special	100	S100	Light Red	Fireplace		A4	firelight effect
S-3	Beam	1000	G40	Straw	behind C.Wnd		C4	sunbeam through window
S-4	Scoop	1000	IF	Lt. Amber	behnd.UL Wnd		C4	genl. sunlight out window
S-5	Beam	500	T64	Medium Blue	behind UL Wd		D4	moonlight through window
T-1	Strip	400	A60	Dk. Magenta	all	1st	D1	tonal lighting
B-1	Strip	200	A40	Flesh Pink	UR backing		B4	light top of stairs
B-2	Scoop	500	IF	Flesh Pink	UL backing		D2	light area outside C.wndo.
B-3	Strip	200	A40	Bast. Amber	DL backing		D3	light area behind door

Figure 68

110 / **Practical Stage Lighting**

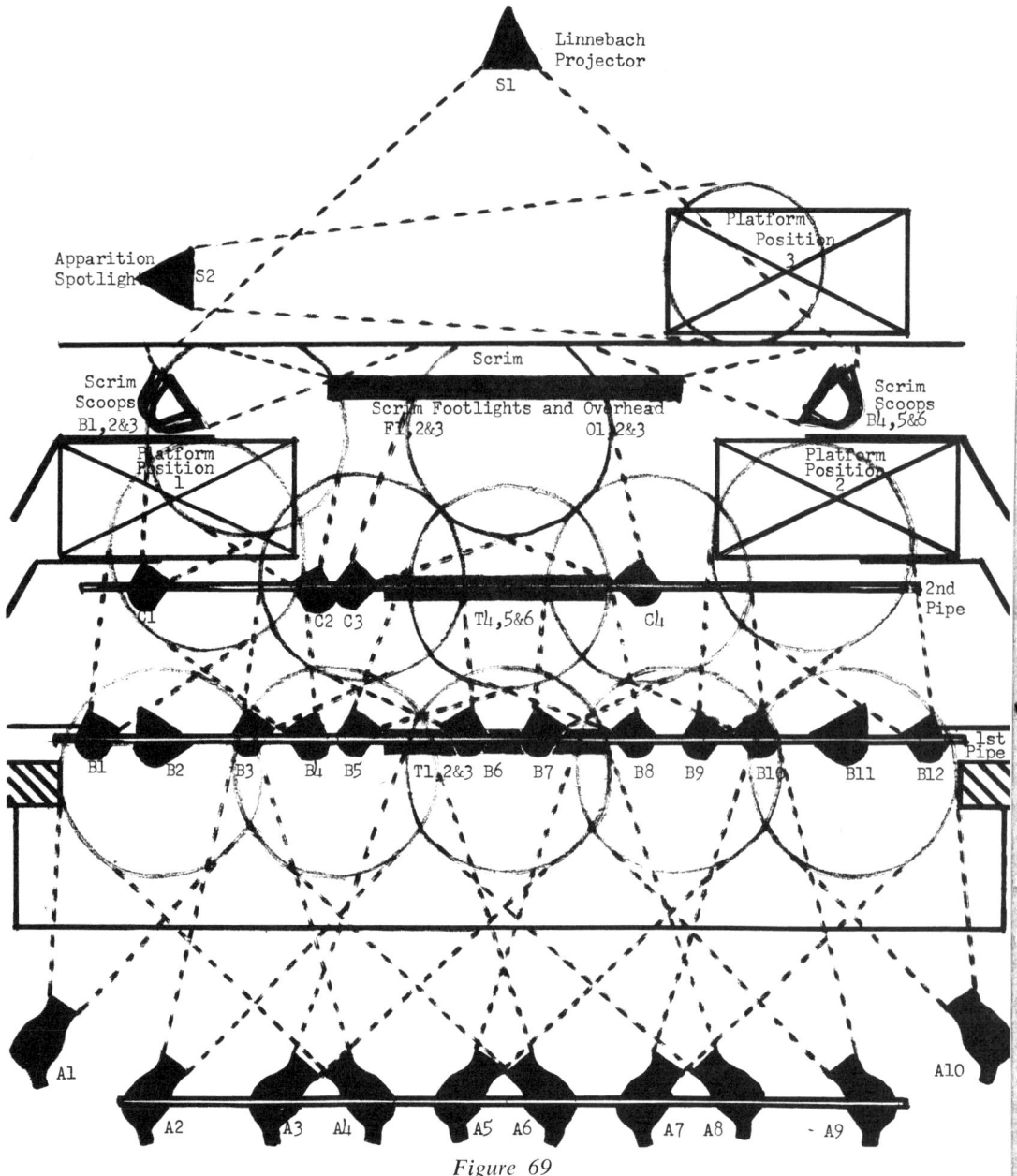

Figure 69

lights that will light the twelve acting areas?
2) How to best obtain the mood and tonal lighting for the scrim and for general area lighting?
3) How to make slides for the new Linnebach projector that was purchased for this production?
4) How to light the UC area in the Troll scene?
5) What special lighting can be used for the apparition scenes?
6) What colors will be used on the acting areas?

It turns out that there is only one problem in the placement of your lighting instruments. By referring to Figure 69 you will see that the house pipe is not long enough to light the DL and DR areas properly. To remedy this, you design two lighting towers that can be easily dismantled and set up. They can stand in the end aisles of the auditorium. They have a telescoping feature that allows you to extend them from 10' high to as high as 18'. They have heavy circular bases 3' in diameter. If you have a good metal shop or maintenance department, they can be built for less than $40 each. They are extremely useful for touring a production and can serve in theatres where there is no house pipe. If necessary, they will hold five lighting instruments each.

Tonal and mood lighting for *Peer Gynt* is quite varied in the various scenes. The Norwegian scenes will require the use of predominantly blue colors. The African scenes will use a predominance of red. In the second production meeting, you discuss mood colors with the director, scene designer, and costumer. All agree that the above mood colors will work well. The director also mentions that he would like a predominance of green for the Troll scene. This meets with agreement from all; in fact, you approve heartily because it gives you an idea for solving the UC acting area problem—but more of that later. One thing is obvious at this point: The mood and tonal lighting should contain all three primary colors. You decide to use borderlights on the first and second pipes and to light the scrim with striplights from above and below. Since you have them available, you use scoops to light the scrim from the sides. Three on each side are sufficient for your 10' scrim. You find that this gives you all of the general lighting you need, except in the Troll scene. The borderlights do not give a high enough intensity of the dense green color to get the desired effect. You solve this problem by placing two large scoops, with green color frames, on the first pipe to supplement the borderlights.

Since this is the major production of the year, your budget still has enough left in it to allow you to buy, from the local hardware, enough sheets of windowpane glass to use as slides for the Linnebach. You get six panes of glass for the following scenic effects:

1. high in the mountains,
2. in the valley,
3. the Hall of the Troll King,
4. the African seacoast,
5. the African desert, and
6. outside the walls of the mental hospital.

To make the slides, you cut your color media in the shapes that you desire (based upon the scene designer's sketches), Scotch tape it to the glass, and project it onto the scrim. You continue to cut and trim until you get the desired effect. In the course of preparing the slides, you find that you only need four slides instead of six. One slide suffices for the mountain top and the valley. You can change from one to the other merely by changing the tilt of the projector so that the mountains are either high or low. The same is true for the African scenes. By raising the tilt, you show the desert sand dunes; by lowering it you get the effect of a desert coastline.

A problem you encounter, however, involves the snowcapped Norwegian mountain peaks. Your original plan was to cut the shape of the mountains and sky so that the bare glass between would represent the snowcapped peaks. When you project this, however, you find that they look like blazing beacons of light dominating the entire picture. You can remedy this by decreasing the intensity of the projector, but this causes the picture you are projecting to fade out also. The best remedy for this problem is to represent the snow by using a gray-colored medium rather than the bare glass.

Another problem you have with the slides is the fact that the projector does not give a clear enough definition to show barbed wire on top of the mental hospital walls. A stereopticon might solve this problem, but the use of one is not feasible, so the designer agrees to forget the barbed wire.

Now we come to the problem of lighting the UC area. This necessitates a special meeting with the director. You ask, first, will the area be used in any scenes other than the Troll scene? He says, "No." Secondly, can you assume that it is primarily to light the Troll King's throne? The answer to this is affirmative. Can it be green light? The director thinks that green will be very effective since the king is the only troll who will not be wearing a mask. In this case, with his particular makeup, green will enhance the effect rather than spoil it. But the director says it must be a lighter green than the background and mood lighting. Your problem is solved.

The scrim lights are green in this scene, the tonal lighting is green. You increase the intensity on the scrim by using a solid green slide in the projector. With all of this green, the lighter green acting area lights will not even be noticeable on the scrim and there will be no washout.

The special light for the apparition presents no problem. A spotlight on an overhead pipe or a pipe stand, with a frost-colored medium will give an apparitionlike appearance when directed on a figure on the platform behind the scrim. This effect may be achieved with the projector on or off. You find that it is more effective if it is accompanied by a decrease in the intensity of the acting area lighting, especially on the left side of the stage (where the apparition is).

The only question left is that of the acting area colors. Of course you have already established the colors for the UC area. You need to select suitable colors for the other areas. Since some of the twelve scenes are light and gay, some are romantic, some are sad, and others are dark and somber, it is impossible to select an overall mood to obtain the best combination of acting area colors. This must be discussed at a production meeting.

The director indicates, first of all, that the light should emanate from right stage in all scenes. The warm color in each acting area will come from the right side. He adds, however, that all of the right areas cannot be the warmest in every scene because he must use the DR area for many of the Buttonmolder's scenes, entrances, and exits. The DR area, then, must be cooler and more sinister. On the other hand, he points out that the warmer scenes and romantic scenes are played chiefly UR and C. This gives you something to work with and you come up with the following plan:

UR—Warm		UC—Green		
R—Warm	RC—Medium	C—Warm	LC—Medium	L—Cold
DR—Cool	DRC—Medium	DC—Medium	DLC—Cool	DL—Cold

With this in mind, you can assign the colors and draw up an instrument schedule as shown in Figure 70.

In touring the production, very few changes had to be made in the lighting. Of the three high schools visited, one had no usable house pipe, and all downstage areas had to be lit from the lighting towers. This created a horizontal angle that was broader than we would have preferred. One high-school stage was only about 20′ deep. We decreased the acting area depth to 12′ allowing an 8′ throw for the projector. This narrowed the projection on the scrim and forced us to move the upstage wings farther onstage in order to mask the unlit scrim. The dancers and crowd scenes were a bit cramped as a result.

Generally, touring improved the lighting. All of the stages were well equipped with borderlights, which were more effective than our portable strips, except that only one of the three schools had a green circuit in their borders. Two of the auditoriums had controls in the projection booth, a luxury that our poor switchboard operators welcomed

#	Type	Wattage	Lamp	Color	Pipe	Use
A1	Ellipsoidal Spot	1000	T12	Flesh Pink	Ho.	DR area
A2	Ellipsoidal Spot	1000	T12	Bastard Amber	Ho.	DRC area
A3	Ellipsoidal Spot	1000	T12	Bastard Amber	Ho.	DC area
A4	Ellipsoidal Spot	1000	T12	Daylight Blue	Ho.	DR area
A5	Ellipsoidal Spot	1000	T12	Light Amber	Ho.	DLC area
A6	Ellipsoidal Spot	1000	T12	Steel Blue	Ho.	DRC area
A7	Ellipsoidal Spot	1000	T12	No Color Pink	Ho.	DL area
A8	Ellipsoidal Spot	1000	T12	Steel Blue	Ho.	DC area
A9	Ellipsoidal Spot	1000	T12	Surprise Pink	Ho.	DLC area
A10	Ellipsoidal Spot	1000	T12	Daylight Blue	Ho.	DL area
B1	Fresnel Spot	500	T20	Medium Amber	1st	R area
B2	Ellipsoidal Flood	1000	G40	Primary Green	1st	Tonal
B3	Fresnel Spot	500	T20	Bastard Amber	1st	RC area
B4	Fresnel Spot	500	T20	Spec. Lavender	1st	R area
B5	Fresnel Spot	500	T20	Straw	1st	C area
B6	Fresnel Spot	500	T20	Steel Blue	1st	RC area
B7	Fresnel Spot	500	T20	Bastard Amber	1st	LC area
B8	Fresnel Spot	500	T20	Surprise Pink	1st	C area
B9	Fresnel Spot	500	T20	No Color Pink	1st	L area
B10	Fresnel Spot	500	T20	Steel Blue	1st	LC area
B11	Ellipsoidal Flood	1000	G40	Primary Green	1st	Tonal
B12	Fresnel Spot	500	T20	Daylight Blue	1st	L area
C1	Fresnel Spot	500	T20	Straw	2nd	UR area
C2	Fresnel Spot	500	T20	Surprise Pink	2nd	UR area
C3	Fresnel Spot	500	T20	Light Green	2nd	UC area
C4	Fresnel Spot	500	T20	Light Green	2nd	UC area
T1	Striplight	240	A60	Primary Red	1st	Tonal
T2	Striplight	240	A60	Primary Blue	1st	Tonal
T3	Striplight	240	A60	Primary Green	1st	Tonal
T4	Striplight	240	A60	Primary Red	2nd	Tonal
T5	Striplight	240	A60	Primary Blue	2nd	Tonal
T6	Striplight	240	A60	Primary Green	2nd	Tonal
F1	Footlight	240	A60	Primary Red	Floor	Cyke
F2	Footlight	240	A60	Primary Blue	Floor	Cyke
F3	Footlight	240	A60	Primary Green	Floor	Cyke
O1	Striplight	240	A60	Primary Red	Cyke	Cyke
O2	Striplight	240	A60	Primary Blue	Cyke	Cyke
O3	Striplight	240	A60	Primary Green	Cyke	Cyke
B1 B4	Ellipsoidal Flood	500	PS30	Primary Red	Stand	Cyke
B2 B5	Ellipsoidal Flood	500	PS30	Primary Blue	Stand	Cyke
B3 B6	Ellipsoidal Flood	500	PS30	Primary Green	Stand	Cyke
S1	Linnebach Project	2000	G48	Slides	Floor	Scrim
S2	Box Spot	500	G30	Frost	Stand	Apparition

Figure 70

with open arms. One stage had their house pipe enclosed behind a solid glass panel in a specially constructed room in the auditorium ceiling, where the technicians could stand and reach the lights at arm level to set and operate them. This was the only stage for which we didn't have to use our light towers. It was a recently built high school with one of the best equipped high-school stages in existence, but the stage floor was constructed of solid concrete.

Now that you know how to prepare a lighting plot, you should be able to set the lights for your production. The next concern is how to run the show. The method of giving cues to the control board operator varies, depending on the theatrical group. You may be given a play script and told to get your cues yourself by hearing or seeing them on the stage. On the other hand, whether or not you can see the stage, you may be required to take all cues from the stage manager or some other person, who will tell you, or give you a hand signal, when each cue is to be made. In some cases this will be done through an intercommunications system or with light signals, called cue lights. Usually a warning is given a minute or two before each cue to alert you and give you a chance to get ready.

If you have a script, mark each cue boldly with a colored marker, using a large "X" to show the exact word or movement that triggers the cue. Identify the cue by cue sheet number, as described below, in the margin of the script. At least one full page before the cue occurs, write in the margin, "WARNING—CUE # ," so that you will be ready for the cue when it comes.

Regardless of how you get your cues, you will need a cue sheet like the one shown in Figure 71. As you can see, it contains several vertical columns each representing a dimmer on your control board. The first column on the left lists the numbers of the cues. Various numbering systems may be used. The most popular system is the use of a letter to designate each scene, followed by a number to show the sequence of each cue

Cue #	Bank "A"				Bank "B"				Bank "C"				Bank "D"			
	1	2	3	4	1	2	3	4	1	2	3	4	1	2	3	4
A-1	9	10	8		8	10	7	6	4	10	4	10	5	10	8	
A-2	Worklights out - 10 sec. dim-out of Houselights															
	CURTAIN															
A-3	Start slow dim to Dusk setting (10 min.) (see A-4)															
A-4	6	8	4		2	7	3	2	5	10	0	1	0	1	0	2
A-5					BLACKOUT - CURTAIN - change gel in S-1											
A-6	Worklights on - Houselights ½ up															
B-1	3	7	8	10	5	8	9	4		10	3		8		6	10
B-2	Worklights out - 5 sec. dim-out of Houselights															
	CURTAIN															
B-3	6	10			6	9							9			
B-4	2	0			0	0	6	7					6		4	
B-5	5 sec. Fade-out to CURTAIN															
B-6	Worklights on - Houselights on															
C-1	10	10	9		8	9	7	6	4	10	4	10	4	10	8	
C-2	Worklights out - 10 sec. dim-out of Houselights															
	CURTAIN															
C-3	0	0	0		0	0	0	0							0	
	Slow CURTAIN															
C-4					10	10	10		(for each curtain call)							
	Worklights on - Houselights on															

Figure 71

Lighting Plots and Cue Sheets / 115

in that scene. For example "A-1" would be the first cue in the first scene and "C-5" would be fifth cue in the third scene. Make sure that you use the same cue numbering system that the person who is giving you the cues is using. In the column opposite each cue number, insert the position of each dimmer for that cue. Most operators prefer to leave the space blank if the dimmer position is not to be changed for that particular cue. The cue sheet in Figure 71 uses that method. The advantage is that you can quickly identify the dimmers you will be using on that cue and need not read the settings of dimmers you will not be using.

You also enter on your cue sheet, on lines between the numbered cues, information concerning any replugging that the operator must do on the interconnecting panel between cues and between acts; or, as may happen with limited facilities, changes of color frames in certain instruments. If a projector is used, changes of slides may also be indicated on the cue sheet. Examples of each of these changes are shown in Figure 71.

If you have a large switchboard, or do not have dimmer group control, you may need two or more switchboard operators. In that case, it will be less confusing if each operator has his own cue sheet showing only the changes that he must make for each cue. If the job is complicated enough, it is frequently advantageous to have a chief operator, with a complete cue sheet, standing behind the operators and checking their cues, possibly lending a hand when needed. Remember, in any case, if you're cramped for space, too many people will only get in one another's way. Two operators who work together well are usually more efficient than four who are stumbling over one another.

It is most important that cues be executed at exactly the right time. Nothing is worse than the awkward pause while an actor waits for the wall switch he is touching to make the lights go on. But even the light changes that are not that obvious to the audience must occur at the instant when they have been planned, because they affect the timing and rhythm of the show. The performances that flop when you can't figure out what went wrong are usually flops because the timing dragged or the rhythm was too erratic.

During rehearsals, do not be ashamed if you get a cue wrong. Request the opportunity to do it over until you get it right. More and more directors, nowadays, set aside a rehearsal, just prior to dress rehearsals, which they call a "technical" rehearsal. The purpose of this rehearsal is for the crews to practice light cues, as well as other technical cues, until the operators can execute them properly. If your director does not use technical rehearsals, try to get him to give you the opportunity to practice cues during the first dress rehearsal. Better yet, if your lights are all set early, ask for permission to practice your lighting cues during some of the regular rehearsal periods.

It is a misconception to think that the need to practice is an indication of a poor operator. On the contrary, the operator who misses cues during a performance because he did not practice enough is really the poor operator.

Appendix A

THE FUNDAMENTALS OF ELECTRICITY

You need not be an electrical engineer to understand what electricity is and how it works. It is taught in every high-school physics course. But we will try not to get even that technical in explaining it. It starts with the atom.

In these days of atom bombs and atomic energy, it is difficult to realize that the majority of the people do not even know what an atom is. So perhaps it is best to begin by defining the atom. If you were to break down any material chemically, the smallest unit that you could isolate is the atom. Each material has its own characteristic atom, and all of the atoms in a given material are the same.

An atom consists of a nucleus and electrons. The electrons travel around the nucleus in orbits, just as the planets in our solar system travel around the sun. The difference between the atoms in one material and those in another rests in the characteristics of their nuclei and in the number of electrons revolving around the nucleus. For instance, the hydrogen atom has only one electron, others have a large number, such as copper, which has twenty-nine electrons. Those twenty-nine electrons do not circle the nucleus each in its own orbit. A great number of them share the same orbit. Some orbits are close to the nucleus, others are farther out. When the outermost orbit contains only one electron, as is true in copper atoms, that electron is easily dislodged from its orbit, whereupon it seeks another atom to become attached to. The more electrons there are in the outermost orbit, the more difficult it is to dislodge any of them.

The characteristic of materials that are good conductors of electricity is that their atoms have very few electrons in the outermost orbit. This is because electricity is actually the movement of those outer-orbit electrons from one atom to another, dislodging one another in a chain reaction. Conversely, materials whose atoms have a large number of electrons in their outermost orbit do not easily dislodge electrons and, therefore, are poor conductors of electricity, or good insulators.

Next, we are concerned with the means of dislodging the electrons to start the flow of electricity. The pressure required to do this is called electromotive force (E.M.F.). The electromotive force is provided by a device that pumps electrons into a conductor in order to push them from atom to atom, through the material, and out the other end where they must reenter the electromotive force device. The most common devices used to provide E.M.F. are the battery and the generator.

Batteries push the electrons through a conductor in one direction only. That movement is called direct current (D.C.). Generators also furnish direct current electromotive force, but they may be designed to push the electrons back and forth in alternating directions. That movement is called alternating current (A.C.). Essentially all household and theatre building electricity in this country is supplied by alternating current generators.

The amount of pressure, or electromotive force, that a battery or generator exerts is measured in terms of volts. A normal flashlight battery generates 2½ volts; most auto batteries, nowadays, generate 12 volts. Household and theatre electricity is generated from an electromotive force of 120 volts, although your kitchen range may be connected with a power line generated by 220 volts. Actually these voltages vary. For instance, 120 volts may actually be anything from 110 to 125 volts. In some localities it is identified as 110 volts, rather than 120. Most manufacturers of electrical equipment will construct their devices for use on 110–120 voltages. Although the difference of 10 or 15 volts is nominal, if you know that your average voltage is higher, or lower, it is safer to use the correct value in making any computations.

Although it is a factor, the electromotive force does not solely govern the rate, or speed, at which the electrons flow through a conductor. The flow of electrons is called the current, or intensity, and it is measured in units called amperes, or amps. One ampere is the amount of current that one volt will push through a given point in a conductor in one second.

The intensity will vary depending upon the amount of resistance that the conductor and electrical devices in the circuit set forth to slow up the current. The resistance is measured in ohms. One ohm is the amount of resistance that will allow one ampere per second to be pushed through a given point in a conductor by one voltage of electromotive force. To illustrate this mathematically, we say:

$$\text{Intensity} = \frac{\text{Electromotive force}}{\text{Resistance}}, \text{ or } I = \frac{E}{R},$$

$$\text{or amperes} = \frac{\text{volts}}{\text{ohms}}$$

That formula is known as Ohm's Law.

We are chiefly interested in the amount of work the electric current can perform. How much power does it furnish to turn our motors, or in our case, to light our lamps? That power is measured in watts, and to determine what it is, we use a formula that has been discussed previously in this book. It is called Watt's Law:

Power = Intensity × Electromotive force, or $P = I \times E$, or watts = volts × amps

Now we have our electromotive force, we have our conductor, and we have our lighting instruments, or devices that perform the work. How can we put them together so that they will work most efficiently? The two types of electrical circuits are the series circuit and the parallel circuit. Their differences depend on how you connect your lighting instruments. Figure 72 shows four lamps connected in a series circuit. Notice that the current must pass through the first light before it goes to the second, and so forth. Because the current flows through each of the resistances successively, the total resistance must equal the sum of all of the individual resistances, or $R_T = R_1 + R_2 + R_3 + R_4$. On the other hand, the current flow must remain the same throughout the circuit, just as when you pull a chain along the ground, each link of the chain moves at the same speed as every other link, so the current is equal at all points, or $I_T = I_1 = I_2 = I_3 = I_4$. In the case of the electromotive force, a portion of it will be used to force the

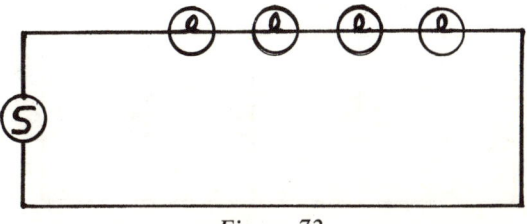

Figure 72

current through each of the resistances successively. This effect is known as a voltage drop, and the entire E.M.F. will be exhausted after the final resistance, or $E_T = E_1 + E_2 + E_3 + E_4$.

Let us see how this works out. Assume that the four lamps connected in series in Figure 72 have resistances of 25 ohms each. Then:

$$R_T = 25 + 25 + 25 + 25 = 100 \text{ ohms}$$

Since the E.M.F. is 120 volts, we can say,

$$I_T = \frac{E_T}{R_T} = \frac{120}{100} = 1.2 \text{ amps}$$

The total current, as well as the current through each lamp, then, is 1.2 amperes. Let us calculate the total voltage drop:

$$\begin{aligned} E_1 = I \times R_1 = 1.2 \times 25 &= 30 \text{ volts} \\ E_2 = I \times R_2 = 1.2 \times 25 &= 30 \text{ volts} \\ E_3 = I \times R_3 = 1.2 \times 25 &= 30 \text{ volts} \\ E_4 = I \times R_4 = 1.2 \times 25 &= 30 \text{ volts} \\ \text{Total Voltage Drop} &= 120 \text{ volts} \end{aligned}$$

A disadvantage of the series circuit is that it causes a voltage drop, which lowers the power, or work performed, for each lamp. Suppose, for instance, we take one lamp out of the circuit. Then:

$$R_T = 25 + 25 + 25 = 75 \text{ ohms, and}$$

$$I_T = \frac{E_T}{R_T} = \frac{120}{75} = 1.6 \text{ amps}$$

Now, let us compare the two situations:

$P = I \times E = 1.2 \times 120 = 144$ watts, with four lamps;

$P = I \times E = 1.6 \times 120 = 192$ watts, with three lamps.

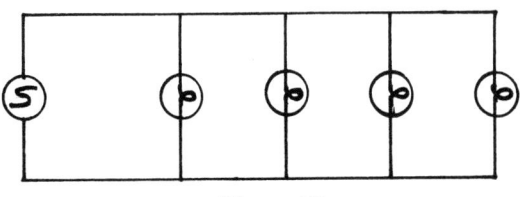

Figure 73

We can, therefore, conclude that the more lights we have in series, the lower the power of each light; and, since $4 \times 144 = 3 \times 192 = 576$, we do not increase the total power by adding more lights.

You have probably figured out another disadvantage in the series circuit merely by looking at Figure 72. You may have had experience with this if you have used Christmas tree lights that were wired in series. When you unscrew one lamp from its socket, you have opened the circuit and stopped the flow of electricity, causing all the rest of the lamps to go out.

Next, let us look at Figure 73, which shows a parallel circuit. In this case, we do not have the chain effect because each of the four lamps forms its own individual, independent circuit. First of all, you can see readily why you can remove any lamp, or lamps, without causing any of the other lamps to go out.

In the parallel circuit the current flows through all of the lamps simultaneously instead of successively and is, therefore, pushed by the full 120 volts at each lamp. We experience no voltage drop. Since the major resistance is created at each lamp, the total resistance will be less than any one of the individual resistances. It is like having one man repair your car on a job that would take him four hours to complete. His rate of work is four hours, but if you had four men working on it simultaneously at the same rate of work (four hours each), the total job would be finished in one hour. The following formula applies:

$$\frac{1}{R_T} = \frac{1}{R_1} + \frac{1}{R_2} + \frac{1}{R_3} + \frac{1}{R_4}$$

Since the voltage remains at 120 volts, we have: $E_T = E_1 = E_2 = E_3 = E_4$, but the current, since we do not have the chain effect, is dissipated as it flows and the total amperage is the sum of each of the individual intensities as they are expended:

$$I_T = I_1 + I_2 + I_3 + I_4$$

If we use the same four 25-ohm lamps, we find:

$$\frac{1}{R_T} = \frac{1}{25} + \frac{1}{25} + \frac{1}{25} + \frac{1}{25} = \frac{4}{25} \quad \text{or}$$

$$4R_T = 25, \quad R_T = 6\tfrac{1}{4} \text{ ohms}$$

Then,

$$I_T = \frac{E_T}{R_T} = \frac{120}{6\tfrac{1}{4}} = 19.2 \text{ amps}$$

$$I_T = 4.8 + 4.8 + 4.8 + 4.8 = 19.2 \text{ amps}$$

If we remove one lamp in this case, we have:

$$\frac{1}{R_T} = \frac{1}{25} + \frac{1}{25} + \frac{1}{25} = \frac{3}{25} \quad \text{or}$$

$$3R_T = 25, \quad R_T = 8.3 \text{ ohms}$$

Then,

$$I_T = \frac{E_T}{R_T} = \frac{120}{8.3} = 14.5 \text{ amps}$$

In comparing those two instances for working power, we find:

$$P = I \times E = 19.2 \times 120 = 2,304 \text{ watts}$$
with four lamps;

$$P = I \times E = 14.5 \times 120 = 1,740 \text{ watts}$$
with three lamps, or three-quarters of the power that you would get using four lamps.

In choosing wire sizes, the following chart may be helpful in deciding how many lights can be used on one cable:

Wire size #	Maximum current	Maximum power at 120 volt E.M.F.
18	3 amps	360 watts
16	6 amps	720 watts
14	15 amps	1,800 watts
12	20 amps	2,400 watts
10	30 amps	3,600 watts

You can see how the $P = I \times E$ formula was used above to convert the amps to watts. You are liable to have to compute the amperage consumption that you have in a given circuit to make sure you do not overload the fused capacity of the circuit. You may use the $P = I \times E$ formula by inverting it so as to determine the maximum amperage. For instance, suppose you want to find what the amperage flow will be in a 120-volt circuit in which you wish to use four 500-watt lamps. We invert $P = I \times E$ to read $I = \dfrac{P}{E}$ and then:

$$I = \frac{4 \times 500}{120} = 16.67 \text{ amps}$$

You know that you can plug these lamps in a circuit that is fused for 20 amps. You should use a #12 size cable, or two #14 size cables with two lights on each cable. You would be courting trouble if you tried to put the four lamps in a circuit that is fused for 15 amps.

Appendix B

SOURCES OF SUPPLY

Theatrical Supply Houses

ALABAMA

The Queen Feature Service, Inc., 2409 First Avenue, Birmingham, 35203

CALIFORNIA

Stagecraft Studios, 1854 Alcatraz Avenue, Berkeley, 94703

Olesen Company, 1535 Ivar Avenue, Hollywood, 90028

COLORADO

Stage Engineering & Supply, Inc., P.O. Box 2002, Colorado Springs, 80901

KENTUCKY

Theatre House, Inc., 115 Sixth Avenue, Dayton, 41074

Falls City Theatre Equipment Co., 427 S. 3 Street, Louisville, 40202

MICHIGAN

Tobins Lake Studios, 2650 Seven Mile Road, South Lyon, 48178

MINNESOTA

Norcostco, 3203 N. Highway #100, Minneapolis, 55422

MISSOURI

Associated Theatrical Contractors, 310 W. 80th Street, Kansas City, 64114

Great Western Stage Equipment, 1324 Grand Avenue, Kansas City, 64106

NEW YORK

Theatrical Services & Supplies, Inc., 411 E. John Street, Lindenhurst, 11757

Art Craft Theatre Equipment, 11 W. 36th Street, New York, 10018

Paramount Theatrical Supplies, 32 W. 20th Street, New York, 10011

Theatre Production Service, 59 Fourth Avenue, New York, 10003

Stagecraft Industries, Inc., 8 Dellwood Road, White Plains, 10606

OHIO

L. & M. Stagecraft, 1634 Walnut Avenue, Cleveland, 44114

Toledo Theatre Supply Co., 3916 Secor Road, Toledo, 43613

PENNSYLVANIA

Atlas Theatrical Equipment, 1517 E. Darby Avenue, Havertown, 19083

Pittsburgh Stage, Inc., 2705 N. Charles Street, Pittsburgh, 15214

TENNESSEE

Knoxville Scenic Studios, 1616 Maryville Pike, S.W., Knoxville, 37901

Tri-State Theatre Supply, 320 S. 2nd Street, Memphis, 38103

TEXAS

Houston Scenic Studios, 7026 Sherman Avenue, Houston, 77011

Richker & Co., 312 Fannin Street, Houston, 77002

Texas Scenic Co., Inc., 1419 Mulberry Avenue, San Antonio, 78201

WASHINGTON

American Theatrical Supply, 2300 1st Avenue, Seattle, 98121

WISCONSIN

Northwest Studios, 2435 Atwood Avenue, Madison, 53704

Midwest Scenic & Stage Equipment, 211 E. Juneau Avenue, Milwaukee, 53202

Electrical Supply Houses

CALIFORNIA

Capitol Stage Lighting, 1451 Venice Boulevard, Los Angeles, 90006

C. W. Cole & Co., Inc., 2560 N. Rosemead Boulevard, South El Monte, 91733

DISTRICT OF COLUMBIA

National Stage Lighting, 925 10th Street, N.W., Washington, 20001

FLORIDA

Jacksonville Stage Lighting, 829 Davis Avenue, Jacksonville, 32202

Bay Stage Lighting Co., 307 S. MacDill Avenue, Tampa, 33609

GEORGIA

Spradlin Bros. Stage Lighting, Mallory Road, Red Oak, 30272

ILLINOIS

Grand Stage Lighting Co., 630 W. Lake Street, Chicago, 60606

Hub Electric Co., Inc., 940 Industrial Drive, Elmhurst, 60126

Midwest Stage Lighting, 2104 Central Avenue, Evanston, 60201

MARYLAND

Winchester Stage Lighting, 301 N. Carey Street, Baltimore, 21223

MASSACHUSETTS

Warren Electric & Hardware Supply Co., 797 Washington Street, Boston, 02111

MINNESOTA

Strand Electric Inc., 3201 N. Highway #100, Minneapolis, 55422

NEW JERSEY

Bash Stage Lighting Co., 407 S. Washington Avenue, Bergenfield, 07621

NEW YORK

Unistage, 330 Genesee Street, Buffalo, 14204

American Stage Lighting Co., 1331c North Avenue, New Rochelle, 10804

Capitol Stage Lighting, 506 W. 56th Street, New York, 10019

Duwico, 250 W. 54th Street, New York, 10019

Packaged Lighting Services, Inc., 36 Woodworth Avenue, Yonkers, 10702

Altman Stage Lighting Co., Inc., 8 Guion Street, Yonkers, 10702

TEXAS

Little Stage Lighting Co., 10507 Harry Hines Boulevard, Dallas, 75220

WASHINGTON

Evergreen Stage & Lighting Co., 23407 Peterson Drive, Mountlake Terrace, 98043

WISCONSIN

Superior Stage Lighting Co., 211 E. Juneau Avenue, Milwaukee, 53202

Lighting Instruments

CALIFORNIA

Berkey Color-Tran, 1015 Chestnut Street, Burbank, 91502

ILLINOIS

Major Equipment Co., 4603 W. Fullerton Avenue, Chicago, 60639

Naren Industries, Inc., 2104 N. Orchard Street, Chicago, 60614

122 / Practical Stage Lighting

NEW JERSEY

Century-Strand, Inc., 3 Entin Road, Clifton, 07014

NEW YORK

Lighting & Electronics, Inc., 81 Prospect Street, Brooklyn, 11201
Genarco, Inc., 15–58 127th Street, Flushing, 11356
Kliegl Bros., 32–32 40th Avenue, Long Island City, 11101
Packaged Lighting Service, Inc., 36 Woodworth Avenue, Yonkers, 10702

OHIO

Strong Electric Corp., 152 City Park Avenue, Toledo, 43601

UTAH

Electro Controls, Inc., 2975 S. 2nd W. Street, Salt Lake City, 84104

Control Equipment

CONNECTICUT

Superior Electric Co., 383 Middle Street, Bristol, 06010
Theatre Techniques, Inc., 60 Connolly Parkway, Hamden, 06514

MASSACHUSETTS

General Radio Corporation, Cambridge (39)

NEW JERSEY

Century-Strand, Inc., 3 Entin Road, Clifton, 07014

NEW YORK

Skirpan Electronics, Inc., 41–43 24th Street, Long Island City, 11101
Ward Leonard Electric Co., 31 South Street, Mount Vernon, 10550

OREGON

Electronics Diversified, Inc., 0625 W. Florida Street, Portland, 97219

UTAH

Electro Controls, Inc., 2975 S. 2nd W. Street, Salt Lake City, 84104

Lamps

MASSACHUSETTS

Sylvania Photolamp Division, 100 Endicott Street, Danvers, 01923

NEW JERSEY

Radiant Lamp Corp., 300 Jeliff Avenue, Newark (8)

NEW YORK

Amplex Corp., 111 Water Street, Brooklyn (1)

OHIO

General Electric Co., Large Lamp Division, Noble Road, Cleveland, 44112

PENNSYLVANIA

Westinghouse Electric Corp., Lamp Division, Union Bank Bldg., Pittsburgh, 15222

Par Lamp Fixtures

NEW YORK

Swivolier Co., Route 304, Nanuet, 10954
General Lighting Co., Inc., 1527 Charlotte Street, New York, 10060

WASHINGTON

Coast Radio Corp., 110 University Avenue, Seattle (1)
Olympic Lighting Co., 8036 45th Avenue, SW, Seattle (16)

Color Media

CALIFORNIA

Berkey Color-Tran, 1015 Chestnut Street, Burbank, 91502

ILLINOIS

Major Equipment Co., 4603 W. Fullerton Avenue, Chicago, 60639

NEW YORK

Gelatin Products Co., 459 Adelphi Street, Brooklyn, 11238

Rosco Laboratories, 214 Harrison Avenue, Harrison, 10528

Kliegl Bros., 32–32 40th Avenue, Long Island City, 11101

Lighting Services, Inc., 77 Park Avenue, New York, 10016 (glass media only)

VERMONT

Brigham Gelatin Co., 17 Weston Avenue, Randolph, 05066

Hardware Supply Houses

ILLINOIS

J. H. Channon Corp., 1447 W. Hubbard Street, Chicago, 60622

MASSACHUSETTS

Levy Hardware Co., Inc., 25 Stuart Street, Boston, 02116

Warren Electric & Hardware Supply Co., 797 Washington Street, Boston, 02111

NEW YORK

Mutual Hardware Corp., 5–45 49th Avenue, Long Island City, 11101

J. R. Clancy, Inc., Syracuse

WISCONSIN

Peter Albrecht Corp., 325 East Chicago Street, Milwaukee, 53202

Cable and Wire

MASSACHUSETTS

Simplex Wire and Cable Co., 63 Sidney Street, Boston

NEW YORK

Rome Wire Co., Rome, 13440

Connectors

CONNECTICUT

Harvey Hubbell, Inc., Bridgeport (2)

NEW YORK

Kliegl Bros., 32–32 40th Avenue, Long Island City, 11101

Templates and Drafting Equipment

ILLINOIS

Lighting Associates, 7817 South Phillips Avenue, Chicago, 60649

Special Effects

CALIFORNIA

Castle Lighting, 1014 N. LaBrea Avenue, Los Angeles, 90038

Tower Electronics, 3421 W. Olive Street, Burbank, 91505

NEW YORK

Times Square Stage Lighting Co., 318 W. 47th Street, New York, 10036

TEXAS

Richker & Co., 312 Fannin Street, Houston, 77002

Black Light Supplies

CALIFORNIA

Ultra Violet Products, Inc., 5114 Walnut Grove Avenue, San Gabriel, 91776

FLORIDA

Strobe Optics, P.O. Box 881, Miami, 33156

NEW YORK

Deelite Blacklite Corp., 7016 20th Avenue, Brooklyn, 11204

Stroblite Co., Inc., 75 W. 45th Street, New York, 10036 (paint only)

Projectors

CALIFORNIA

Christie Electric Corp., 3412 W. 67th Street, Los Angeles, 90043

OHIO

Jones Projector, 2727 6th Avenue, Cuyahoga Falls, 44221

BIBLIOGRAPHY

Alcone Co. *Paramount Theatrical Supplies Catalog No. 11*. New York.

Bellman, Willard F. *Lighting the Stage: Art and Practice*. Chandler Publishing Co., San Francisco. 1967.

Bowman, Wayne. *Modern Theatre Lighting*. Harper & Brothers, New York. 1957

Burris-Meyer, Harold and Cole, Edward C. *Scenery for the Theatre*. Little, Brown and Co., Boston. 1947.

Century-Standard, Inc. *Memo-Q * Literature*. Clifton. 1969.

Fuchs, Theodore. *Stage Lighting*. Little, Brown and Co., Boston. 1929.

Heffner, Hubert C., Seldon, Samuel, and Sellman, Hunton D. *Modern Theatre Practice,* 4th edition. Appleton-Century-Crofts, New York. 1959.

Miller, James Hull. *Small Auditoriums With Open Stages*. Hub Electric Co., Inc., Elmhurst. 1969.

———. *Little Theatres From Modest Spaces*. Hub Electric Co., Inc., Elmhurst. 1962.

Parker, W. Oren and Smith, Harvey K. *Scene Design and Stage Lighting,* 2nd edition. Holt, Rinehart & Winston, New York. 1968.

Seldon, Samuel and Sellman, Hunton D. *Stage Scenery and Lighting,* rev. edition. F. S. Crofts & Co., New York. 1943.

Simon, Bernard. *Simon's Directory of Theatrical Materials Services & Information,* 3rd edition. Package Publicity Service, New York. 1966.

Sylvania Division. *Lighting Handbook for Television, Theatre, Professional Photography,* 3rd edition. General Telephone & Electronics, Danvers. 1969.

---

* Patent pending.